NEW AND COLLECTED POEMS

CLIVE WILMER was born in Harrogate in 1945, grew up in London and was educated at King's College, Cambridge. He now teaches English at Cambridge, where he is a Fellow of Sidney Sussex College, a Bye-Fellow of Fitzwilliam College and an Honorary Fellow of Anglia Ruskin University. He has published five Carcanet collections of poetry, as well as one volume with the Worple Press, *The Falls* (2000). Clive Wilmer is an authority on John Ruskin and his contemporaries, and has edited selections of Ruskin, William Morris and, for Carcanet's Fyfield series, Dante Gabriel Rossetti. He is the Master of the Guild of St George, the charity founded by Ruskin in 1871. He has edited the essays of Thom Gunn and, in two Carcanet volumes, Donald Davie. With George Gömöri, he has translated widely from modern Hungarian poetry, notably the works of Miklós Radnóti and György Petri. In 2005 he was awarded the annual Pro Cultura Hungarica Medal for translation by the Hungarian Ministry of Culture. An occasional broadcaster, he fronted BBC Radio 3's *Poet of the Month* programmes and his interviews are published by Carcanet as *Poets Talking*.

Also by Clive Wilmer from Carcanet Press

Poetry
The Dwelling Place
Devotions
Of Earthly Paradise
Selected Poems 1965–1993
The Mystery of Things

Translation
(with George Gömöri)
Miklós Radnóti, *Forced March: Selected Poems*

Editions
Dante Gabriel Rossetti, *Selected Poems and Translations*
Donald Davie, *With the Grain*
Donald Davie, *Modernist Essays*

Interviews
Poets Talking: The 'Poet of the Month' Interviews from BBC Radio 3

CLIVE WILMER

New and Collected Poems

CARCANET

First published in Great Britain in 2012 by
Carcanet Press Limited
Alliance House
Cross Street
Manchester M2 7AQ

www.carcanet.co.uk

Translations from the revised edition of Miklós Radnóti, *Forced March*
(Enitharmon Press, 2003) are included by kind permission of the publisher.

A CIP catalogue record for this book is available from the British Library

ISBN 978 1 84777 052 3

The publisher acknowledges financial assistance from Arts Council England

Supported by
ARTS COUNCIL
ENGLAND

Typeset by XL Publishing Services, Tiverton
Printed and bound in England by SRP Ltd, Exeter

To Patricia

What thou lovest well remains,
                              the rest is dross
What thou lov'st well shall not be reft from thee
What thou lov'st well is thy true heritage

EZRA POUND

When we build, let us think that we build for ever. Let it not be for present delight, nor for present use alone; let it be such work as our descendants will thank us for, and let us think, as we lay stone on stone, that a time is to come when those stones will be held sacred because our hands have touched them, and that men will say, as they look upon the labour and wrought substance of them, 'See! this our fathers did for us.'

JOHN RUSKIN

CONTENTS

KING ALFRED'S BOOK & OTHER POEMS (1992–2000)

I

II   *Three Epistles*

III

IV

THE MYSTERY OF THINGS (2006)

I

II

REPORT FROM NOWHERE & OTHER POEMS (2006–2011)

I

II

III

POEMS WRITTEN FOR SIDNEY SUSSEX COLLEGE, CAMBRIDGE
(2009–10)

ACKNOWLEDGEMENTS

Carcanet Press, I am happy to say, has been publishing my work for thirty-five years. This book brings together most of the four collections they have issued, and two new ones. The first of the new ones, *King Alfred's Book & Other Poems*, comprises the eleven 'New Poems' from my Carcanet *Selected Poems* (1995) and seventeen poems from *The Falls*, which was published by the Worple Press in 2000. The second, *Report from Nowhere & Other Poems*, consists of twenty-three previously unpublished poems written over the last five years. I have also revived eight poems omitted from earlier volumes: 'The Long Climb', the 'Two Cambridge Images', 'A Plaque', 'The River in Springtime', 'The Translator's Apology', 'Greensleeves' and 'The Source'. I have inserted these where they might have appeared in the books from which I originally excluded them. A few poems cropped up in more than one of my collections – 'Wild Flowers', 'Bindweed Song', 'An Autumn Vision', 'Visitation', 'The Holy of Holies, 'A Vision', 'W.S. Graham Reading', 'The Falls' – so had to be fixed in one collection here. I have made a few revisions, but all of them are minor adjustments; I have made no substantial changes. I have also corrected some mysterious typographical errors that disfigured my *Selected Poems*.

In addition to my own poems I have included a large selection from my work as a translator. The thirty-six translations from Hungarian were all produced in collaboration with George Gömöri, with whom I have been working for nearly forty years and to whom I owe an enormous debt. Our versions from Miklós Radnóti were first published as *Forced March* (Carcanet, 1979). A new edition, revised and expanded, was published by the Enitharmon Press in 2003; all the Radnóti poems reprinted here are from that edition. Most of the poems by György Petri are taken from *Eternal Monday: Selected Poems* (Bloodaxe Books, 1999), those by George (or György) Gömöri himself from *Polishing October: New and Selected Poems* (Shoestring Press, 2008) and those by János Pilinszky from *Passio: Fourteen Poems* (Worple Press, 2011). The poems by Anna T. Szabó were published in the *Hungarian Quarterly*, as were three uncollected poems by Petri; those by Jenő Dsida, István Vas and Domokos Szilágyi were anthologised in *The Colonnade of Teeth:*

Modern Hungarian Poetry, edited by George Gömöri and George Szirtes (Bloodaxe Books, 1996).

The book includes a few commissioned pieces. The two poems written for Sidney Sussex College, Cambridge, where I am a Fellow in English, have both been set to music: the 'Valedictory Ode' for Dame Sandra Dawson by James Freeman and 'The Sidney Carol' by Christopher Page. Both were sung in Chapel by the College choir and have since been published in the *Sidney Sussex College Annual*. 'Caedmon of Whitby' was written as the libretto for John Hopkins's *Cantata*, commissioned by BBC Radio 3 in 1993. 'Epitaph' has been carved on the gravestone of my late friend Michael Bulkley in Histon Road Cemetery, Cambridge. 'Bottom's Dream' was commissioned for *Around the Globe*, the magazine of Shakespeare's Globe Theatre. 'Civitas' was commissioned by Magdalene College, Cambridge, for its Festival of Landscape in 2009 and published in the festival anthology: *Contourlines: New Responses to Landscape in Word and Image*, edited by Neil Wenborn and M.E.J. Hughes (Salt Publishing, 2009).

Many items in this *Collected Poems* now appear in a book for the first time. Most of them were first published in the following magazines, to whose editors my thanks are due: *Agenda*, *Around the Globe*, *Hungarian Quarterly*, *Modern Poetry in Translation*, *Notre Dame Review*, *PN Review*, *Poetry*, *Port*, *The London Magazine*, *Times Literary Supplement*.

Clive Wilmer

from

THE DWELLING-PLACE
(1977)

IN MEMORY OF MY FATHER

A man's religion is the form of mental rest, or dwelling-place, which, partly, his fathers have gained or built for him, and partly, by due reverence to former custom, he has built for himself; consisting of whatever imperfect knowledge may have been granted, up to that time, in the land of his birth, of the Divine character, presence, and dealings; modified by the circumstances of surrounding life.

JOHN RUSKIN, *Val d'Arno*

I

The Exile

I threw up watchtowers taller than my need
With bare walls the enemy could not scale,
I wrenched stone from the near countryside
And built my city on the highest hill;
    Over the land I scarred I reared
Impenetrable the walls and citadel.

Then to approach the city from afar
All you could see was soaring, there was such peace
Knowing the city mine I lay secure.
My own, one night, woke me – every face
    A jutting rock relief in glare,
The torchlight that illumined new distress.

They lit me into darkness. The harsh sun –
My understanding dazzled when it dawned –
Disclosed me vulnerable. I stumbled on,
Till blown, a sterile seed, by years like wind
    Indifferent guidance, I am set down
Among familiar stone in a changed land.

Now it is only details I perceive:
The towers lopped, stone interspersed with weed
In patches; a deeper speckling seems to give
Form to the complex of decay, but is fled
    With a lizard flicker. Poppies revive,
In the wall they spatter, spectres of old blood.

Chiaroscuro

Chiaroscuro: abandoned dark
Falling back before the advancing light.
If the room I live in were not so vast
The light I hold would cancel the black
Out there, that dissipates my range of sight.

To banish darkness, first you must plumb
The darkness' depth – and nothing known more deep.
I know true darkness is much more
Than interrupted light – shadow clung
To the thing's edge – or the domain of sleep.

I have known times when the mind cracks before
The force of its own thoughts. With those
Moments in mind he has taken a lamp
To cast a light on the future's flickering floor;
Behind his back, the gates of darkness close.

Behind his back, the gates of darkness close;
The leap he takes is into light's abyss,
Knowing that at the brink one never knows
Whether it's darkness that encloses
Light, or the light darkness.

He takes a chance on what may lie in store
For him in landscapes where the objects glow:
In my world where the darkness breeds around me,
Light may open up a world beyond me.
Opening outward, opening more and more.

The Invalid Storyteller

Lace, we remember, faded lace
To filter light and veil the panes
   Against the external day.
The light was intermeshed with lace
Upon the wall, fastidious,
In patterns subtle as decay
   And intricate as pain:
Like pinks and greens on carcasses,
Like wrinkles on an old man's face.

Beyond our reach, above the veil
Where knowledge knit with pain and death
   Shimmered, the sun's rays
Burst through the panes and cast a pale
Rectangular frieze upon the wall,
Whose colours told of summer days,
   Whose pallor told of death;
Where he could watch what he recalled
Advancing, as he told each tale.

The Sparking of the Forge

Stiffened and shrunk by age my grandfather
Leans forward now, confined within his chair,
Straining to raise a finger to point back
Over his shoulder, scarcely able to look
Over his shoulder through the darkening window
At the road behind him and before me where

The mailcoach ran just seventy years ago –
He suddenly tells me, reaching to capture one
Glimpse of the road where memory finds its form
And in whose lamps so many memories burn:
The armed guard in the rear, behind bars –
Changing the horses at the road's end inn –

And where we buy his tobacco every day
Was once the blacksmith's forge. I watch him stare
Into the crumbling coal and feel the blaze
Flare in the ancient forge and his childhood-eyes;
And whether the shoes were hammered on red-hot
Uncertain now, he recollects their glare.

His words uncertain now I watch him see
Bright in his mind the sparking of the forge,
The monstrous anvil and the sizzling steel,
The raising of the hammer high to feel
What once he had of muscle in his arm,
The hammer's beat sounding his deepest urge.

Each time recalled another fragment lost,
Still his past seeps back – with broken breath –
Continuous in a stream of memories.
I pick up only broken images:
Confined by time, as he is by his age,
My own time's loss I find in his lost youth.

An old man's death becomes a young man's rage;
I seize the coal-tongs; now the blacksmith's clamp
Shadows my tiny room with smouldering giants,
An arm is raised to fall which, falling, hurls
Hammer-blows forward rung with resonance;
And, shod with steel now, hear the hard hoof stamp.

East Anglian Churchyard
for Robert Wells

The land low-lying – the fen drained –
Still partakes of the flood, and the soil
Of this green graveyard still has the swell,
The broken swell, of a calm sea, beneath which
Graves are submerged.

And this church – dateless, its wall at a lean
And no tower – is a beached ship,
Perhaps of northern pirates who having no more
Rich coastal abbeys to fire, settling,
Passed from the blue.

From the deep half-salvaged, there is one tombstone
That rears above the surface where leaf-light swims
In the shade of an oak-tree, ageless, ivied –
The stone entwined by the same ivy, its name
Blotted by moss.

Beside recent deaths, no other stone
In sight – though here and there, a vague swell
Covers a forgotten life. This
Particular spot in the shade, he must have
Chosen for memory.

Genealogy: The Portrait

Born in India where the sun glared
at the stoical English; his father's lip
stiff under the huge moustache, knit
with grizzled whiskers over the stiff
gilding of his red coat's collar; his mother,
haughty, decked in imperial silks,
her boned collar; the father's hands
so massive, sinewed and scarred and no
soft lulling at the mother's breast:
a Victorian childhood, steel grey.

Sent back home to England: for hard
study and games under threat of the birch,
the runs before breakfast, the cold baths:
to make a man of him.
                    And in his manhood
(before the Depression's grime, old age
and death) unfit for the Great War, tall
in Edwardian grey, a slight physique;
and his pale, melancholy, liberal eyes
fade from the picture looked at two wars past
by his son, who has no children, and remembers.

Victorian Gothic
for Dick Davis

Blackened walls: a Gothic height
Crouches and does not soar, locked
To the earth like slabs of outcrop stone
That touch no God; they imitate

Monoliths of the moors. Smokebound
Maze of streets in a northern town,
Low-skied misted marshland: ghosts
Haunt him, a grave imagination.

Mist merged with industrial smoke
Where the ghosts swim:
Their scrawny bodies topped with blackened heads
Like those that peer through jungle leaves.

Manufacturers, poets, moralists, colonisers, all
Engendered empires of despair
Built on blackness in the grey air.

What does the grey stone mask? Such battlements
Attest obscure defence.
                              His mind draws
Close to its melancholy: as
In dank winter to the heaped log-fire
Of a Saxon hall, beyond whose walls
What lurks in greyness?

Castles from dark days his reason
Girdles like siege but preserves,
Long years of siege that constitute defence;
Renascence ghosts, dark blood
Steams on the axe – industrial fumes
Dry the blood of the starved worker – marshland
Dank at sunset the sky bleeds
Pillarbox red.

The Ruined Abbey

And now the wind rushes through grassy aisles,
And over the massy columns the sky arches.

The monks who built it
Were acquainted with stone and silence.
Knowing the grandeur and endurance
Of isolated winter oaks, of rock,
And the hard rhythms of moors,
They retired here and reared it
From the crust of the north, moulding this form
Around their core of silence.

Their minds were landscaped.
Not with summer gardens that give sense ease
Nor beaches that lull questionings to a doze.
Their landscapes asserted agonies that
Probed them to the nerve;
The hardness of rock and the stream's ice
Formed a resistance they learned to resist,
To subdue, till it yielded
To silent movements of joy –
To the penetrating warmth of a mellow sun,
Its venerable eye.

The streams locked by ice,
The rocks, and the edged wind
Resisted their cowled will to define.
But resistance tautened questionings whose sinew
Shaped understandings.
The moor's silence snowed meanings,
And they knew that, while ice melts or cracks, they
Could endure like the rocks.

And so from the stone of landscaped minds, they fashioned
A form for those meanings, a form
That arched over meaningful air.
According to their time they shaped it

With massive grace.
And in the face of evil, weathers and decay
Its essence constant in the shiftings of ages.

And now the wind rushes through the grassy aisles,
And over the massy columns the sky arches.

In ruin, the form remains;
When the form falls, there is stone;
Stone crumbled, there is still
The dust, dust… and a silence
The centuries bow to – a silence
Lapped by the speechless howl of winds.

Yorkshire, the West Riding, 1965

The Long Climb

not that run
into the candled darkness
with light enough for you not
to see your sins by –
light enough
to daze you with a beauty that does not speak
of the long struggle, but rather

climbing winding stairs
to the top of an ancient tower, so tall
it seems to have no end –
    and less light there, the turning
in narrowest confines, and
asperity of cold stone –

where the small light calls to a search
for the more there may be, the climb no
perversely tortuous
fascination lit with glimmers –
    abrasion, this is it, you can
crack your skull in the dark on stone, graze
blood-points from the skin, fall even
in sprawled confusion, but this

is where life touches – where blood
run to the head, the heart
beats to its peril – and there is for you
(unable to see round corners)
no end
to the long climb

unless you should reach the top –
from the start your aim though lost
often enough
when your only thought was climbing –
and from it see

spread out before you the whole of it

when the eye goes journeys
league upon league over land
in the clear sun, light that

hardens edges yet
infuses all with itself
is strong, this

(if at all you reach it
if it be there)
this is the vision

Florence, 1968

The Well

All day to gaze down into a well
as into yourself – as through self
to the blue sky fringed with green

of the world; and at length,
through a tunnelled forest of fronds that grow
from the mossy walls, to perceive

only your own face against the sky,
eyes glazed in contemplation, staring back
through a forest: is at large

to behold and desire to behold –
through foliage and from beyond darkness –
always, as in a well, meeting your stare,

your own face afloat on the surface,
with your thoughts bubbling from the deep spring
and your voice, reverberant, echoing response;

and to forget how without it
there is only the old perspective into endless dark
with silence at the source.

II

The Dedication
E.W., 1882–1948

It was your room they moved me to
   (I, not yet four the year you died,
    Not grasping how I might have cried),
Dear Father, whom I hardly knew;

And your great, polished chest-of-drawers
   Was all that I inherited
    Besides: it loomed above my bed:
Dark in the wood-grain still there pours,

In memory, vast, the gathered deep –
   Huge waves that surged, curded to foam
    (In the security of home),
And broke, as I sank into sleep.

Clearing the drawers out, now a man,
   I came upon your photograph:
    It seemed a visual epitaph
To one I'd never thought, till then,

I'd loved or feared. Now time had blurred
   Your placid features, void of care,
    Who died, as if you had no heir,
Intestate: so on me conferred

No such authority as dressed,
   In my conception, all your acts;
    Mere rooms to occupy as facts –
No freehold rightfully possessed.

Moreover, childish hands, untaught
   In every art but innocence,
    Had scribbled into radiance
The aspect which the lens had caught

And overlaid its sepia hue –
    Your clothes now black and gold, your face
    Crimson, the sky (your dwelling-place)
Empty but touched with purest blue –

As if a fatherless naïf,
    Dreaming a different element,
    Within the oval frame had meant
To translate his confused belief

Into pictorial commentary:
    This was the palimpsest I'd scrawled
    Glimpsing a King, beyond my world,
Who governed from across the sea.

Your power you held but to resign –
    A rationally gentle reign;
    I see you smiling, mild again,
Whose failing life engendered mine;

And through my childhood dreams, that face
    Taught what a child could never see:
    That I must never hope to be
The master of my dwelling-place.

1975

The Rector
Naturalist, poet, priest (1753–1830)

    Privation for the poor
    Was want of a shared soul,
And hungry intellect was stripped
    Of serviceable role,

When in that partial Eden
   The guardian of the Word
Had died, their pastor, who had named
   The creatures of the Lord.

   For the Word formed his thought,
   His task to make collation
Of scripture with what quickened it,
   The other book, Creation;

   And to the inward order
   Thus answered, testify
In prose whose measured harmony
   Compassed the butterfly;

   Or verse that singled out
   Familiar things, which could
From prospect near or far reveal,
   In them, a primal good:

   The truth he sought. Such fortune!
   For love could move the search,
Till all that his attention held
   Attended on his church

   And drew toward the walls
   Thick creepers still embrace,
Where chastened by the sombre yew
   Light haunts his resting-place.

   There once, a kind of pilgrim,
   I thought how sad and mean
(Being shrunken to that yard and grove)
   Was his once-fair demesne

   And seeing the gravestones
   As fragments of his store
I felt from hedgerow, evening air
   And stream his spirit soar

But met him in my own
  Unsanctuaried spirit
Among the stones of an estate
  I never shall inherit.

Arthur Dead

Terror stalks this land where once King Arthur
    Ruled with virtue steeped in vision;
Now in restless vigil his knights quest, their impulse
    Dark obsession.

Yet those few, who halting at the wayside
    Kneel to victims of the terror,
Salvage thus, from desolation which they ride in,
    Love and honour.

In Malignant Times

1. *In Time of Civil War*

A doctor: for the time's disease
He knew no cure: though he could ease
This mind's unrest, that body's pain.
The makeshift home where he was sane
Housed tranquil dignity, that bore
Sober mistrust for holy war.

The war he died in was not his:
Between two equal enemies
He chose to work withdrawn. But when
Ordered to sacrifice those men –
Patients and friends – who shared his home,
He chose to fight the war, alone.

Scorning promiscuous rhetoric,
With chaste formality he spoke:
The abstract words of his defence
Were tempered by experience,
No more: beyond that point he chose
The silence of secure repose.

2. *On a Lutheran Pastor who Preached against Hitler*

Ein feste Burg ist unser Gott

The time's demons had all but quelled
The faith he taught, to which he held
In doubt and hope. So he withdrew
To preach a version of the true:
Exiled within reality
To mediate lost sanctity.

When a Black Death of the spirit broke
Over Europe in blood and smoke
And silence, his truth named as fact
What lucid empiricism lacked
Scope to envisage. A stronghold still
For him, his faith embraced the real.

His speech was action. The long quest
Of Europe's centuries seems compressed
Behind those words: which yet contain
In their calm voice his insight's pain;
Which drove hysteria and pride
Beyond the clearing where he died.

Likeness

In John the Pisan's statue, at Siena,
Of the wolf suckling Romulus and Remus,
In the anxious eyes and searching nose – the low
Thrust of her gaunt head from the prominent spine,

I see my own dog: she, though sweetly pampered,
Looked drained and scrawny when, still half a puppy,
With bleeding teats, she bowed beneath her instinct
To mother her first brood: I see this much

As he, the sculptor, must have seen the she-wolf
And every burden dour fate lays on us
In the bent head of a spurned mongrel bitch
Upon the streets of Pisa or Siena.

The Goldsmith

To stay anxiety I engrave this gold,
Shaping an amulet whose edges hold
A little space of order: where I find,
Suffused with light, a dwelling for the mind.

Sanctuary
Torcello Cathedral

On the massive grey stone shutters (by stone rings
Hinged to the Roman windows of the church walls)
Are scars that might be some wedged archaic script –
Through time obscured, through history part-deciphered.

Brooding on these, we conjure a day of trouble
When a mudflat, where grass grows amid brackish fens,
Grew from the mist, a blurred hope, barely risen
From the grey, tideless sleep of the lagoon.

For them though, a clear space, between fear and the sea:
For – the last walls of their larger fortress, Empire,
Fallen to Northern barbarians, to the Lombards –
They had fled to sea: to build their hopes on sand.

There from the crude substance of memories and images
And marble salvaged from the waste that was once their home,
They hewed a temple, draining the land around it:
Sowed crops there, bred beasts, drew fish from the sea.

And raised a high tower reaching above the mist,
Bell-tower and watch-tower, over the sea's languor:
And marine-dull chimes from the bell that called to prayer
Would call to safety women children and cattle

Into the fortress of their sanctity.
Then doors were barred and the slabs rolled over the windows
To bear their silent witness to Eastern arrows,
And the men went out to confront their older adversary:

Not purgers of decadence – the indifferent offspring
Of history, whose molten rush is cast in words –
But immemorial, grey ghost-marauders
That broke on the shore, grey spume of the ancient sea.

The Disenchanted

On a painting by Atkinson Grimshaw, 'Liverpool Quay by Moonlight' (1887)

Riding at anchor ships from the New World,
Cargo-less now, sway, as in a trance;
Their lights float on a mist, their sails are furled;
They have disembarked both energy and distance.

Fated by deep unrest to haunt the quay
Aimless pilgrims, lit by the blear gaslight,
Emerge from haze, withdrawn in reverie:
       Exiles from day and night.

And at shop-windows they become transparent
To golden light that charms the brazen riches
There on display, before which they lament –
       As at vain reliquaries

That hold dead sanctity. They stare at distance
Imported by a manufactured world
To allure their wasting energy and substance
       By turning all to gold.

Bewitched but disenchanted lords they are,
Of a legendary treasure long since dispossessed,
Who drift with the dissolving atmosphere –
       Dim shades of the lost.

Only the lamp on a black advancing coach
– Unearthly green! – can focus in reflection,
Composing all you see as you approach:
Light of the mind it stays from desolation.

Bird Watcher

It returns to the same nest. The watcher lies
Beneath spring brushwood to await its coming –
At watch so long he dreams himself becoming
Less than himself and more, the landscape's eyes.

Though far beyond his eyes, beyond the range
Of field-glasses, he knows it breaks no bonds:
Its instinct to his knowledge corresponds,
Riding the current of the season's change.

What is there in a small bird's blood that learns
To plot its course by sun and stars, being drawn
Yearly toward a lost, remembered dawn?
The watcher broods on this. The bird returns.

And all its colours flash where he attends –
A deep blue mantling rust and white. It sings
Caged in his retina; then on curving wings
Veers off to vanish where the human ends.

Saxon Buckle
in the Sutton Hoo treasure

His inlaid gold hoards light:
A gleaming thicket to expel,
With intricacy worked by skill,
The encroaching forest night
Where monsters and his fear dwell.

Gold forest tangles twined by will
Become a knot that closes in
The wild beasts that begin
Beyond his habitation.
An object for his contemplation,

From which three rivets gaze:
A beast's head forested within,
That clasps his swordbelt to his waist
By daylight, and before his eyes,
By hearthlight, stills unrest.

from

DEVOTIONS

(1982)

TO DIANE

Love, these are shapes of nothing, but they took
Time from our love, and time can never give
Of its own self again; so take my book,
This witness to an absence where I live.

I

The Advent Carols

Aspiciens a longe

I look from afar. We stand in darkness.
A people in exile, shall we hear good news,
Who toward midnight, in mid-winter, sing?

Sing words to call a light out of the darkness
To thaw dulled earth, to unfold her fairest bud;
Our song holds faith that the Word will be made flesh.

Now we bear candles eastward, bear them into
Inviolate dark the Word should occupy:
Light disembodied swells the sanctuary

Where an old dream is mimed, without conviction,
Over again. I look from afar. Our sung words
Are herald angels, and they announce his name,

But lay no fleshly mantle on the King,
The one Word. And yet, in the song's rising
Is rapture, and dayspring in the mind's dark:

For the one sanctuary, now, is the word not
Made flesh – though it is big with child, invaded
By the dumb world that was before it was.

Narcissus, Echo

Only reflection sanctifies,
For him, the beauty she holds dear.

She calls and calls to him, till all
The vacant world resounds with love.

My Great Aunt, Nearing Death

Her narrow life has straitened to this room.
Arranged like a saint's corpse in a reliquary –
Hands clasped
Over her virgin womb –
Her body lies,
Trusting that soon the hand of love will find her.
Blind eyes
Focused on all or nothing.

Her life has known naïve gentility
Only and so one thought that that defined her.
Yet charity
(Her visitors bear witness),
Though she is poor, is in her daily gift –
So call it love.

Blind hands –
Ignorant both of passion and of harm,
Hands she can barely lift –
With gentleness, conferring calm,
Reach out to where my little children stand:
They who, like her, fear nothing,
Doubt no love.

On the Demolition of the 'Kite' District
Cambridge, 1980

On the smashed hearthstone or the fallen lintel
Carve words to witness:
                    That men who called themselves
Conservatives, lying in their teeth, tore down
Good rooms, good walls of weathered brick, erasing
A wordless register of birth and death.

Il Palazzo della Ragione

Passing the central Palace (called 'of Reason')
In Padua, daily I'd contemplate,
High on one wall among begrimed inscriptions,

Leaning as from a window, a gentleman
In Quattrocento costume – with a turban.
He smiles across distance, his hand raised in greeting.

Smiling as if at me, to bid me welcome
To a city, enlightened and humane,
Whose style I can neither touch nor imitate.

And though I would not say
This is a final wisdom,
As of Christ or the Buddha, on the Palace of Reason,

Yet it seems he has a graciousness
Beyond our time to emulate,
Though one may celebrate.

That smile across the ages is intent
On courtesy. And none the less,
I suffer it as though it were contempt.

Pony and Boy

the pony presses
its muzzle into the bark
of the tree blindly
as my boy, across the stream
leaning towards it, gazes

Two Cambridge Images

1. *The Market-Place at Midnight*

No moon,
but lamp light.

The fountain dead,
planks fallen.

Row upon row, still,
of stalls:
crude boards roped across
trestles, and slack canvas.

2. *Michaelmas Term, 1964*

   On gleaming flagstones
cold rain falls
            Young men walk
above the stores of vintage
         to the library

1968, 1979

Beyond Recall
for Thom Gunn

Imprecision of the senses at midday:
stirred,
      having been struck
by the sharp bitter-sweet of a new wine
drunk in a clouded bar
                   – where
to nose and tongue came the tang
of pickled onions, of briny olives and, raw
to the back of the throat, the reek
of cheap cigar smoke.

               Light
on crude gems that define a haze.
They, once possessed – though precious
beyond recall – remain his
alone
      who inclining toward the past
hears nightingales in the dark, yet never can
transcribe their fluid melodies.

II

from Air and Earth

Migrant

O Redwing,
with your slashed sleeves, with
your speckled breast, the livid
stripe on your brow –

how you must stand out
against
the Iceland tundra – white
or grey – as with a
stain of your warm blood;
yet here

accommodate yourself
to songthrush and mild lawn,
and to that snow
of the new season: may,
streaking the hawthorn hedge.

Beside the Autobahn

It is sunk deep, this
motorway

       And all along it,
where the rats and mice –
now vulnerable, since they
cannot undermine a
causeway through their territory –
must cross,
       there perch
on fence-posts, nothing moved,
these long-eared owls
who wait

     As,
through millennia, owl
eyes have to the dusk become
enlightened:
         even so those ears,
to patterings
beneath the passing traffic, are
attuned

Aerial Songs

i

from his high perch
Thrush
sings the morning, from

an aerial
upon a chimney-stack –
above
the abstract foliage.

More than a
plump, warm,
speckled, dust-brown
body – he's

a voice
awakening the city
folk
    to what
daily lost but eternal
hour of the incipient.

The tree he has alighted
on was neither
born nor dies: so he
recurs

ii

likewise, at dusk,
Blackbird his brother:
plumage
            losing
in the dark – his bright bill
sings
the sun to setting.

And the air is his!
                    For us,
        that song
articulates
the space that was
before towns were.
                    It heralds,
retrospectively,
                    the sunk
emergence of our dwellings
from the greenwood –
                    from the green
world, dark and other.

For his bill is golden,
though the wings are swart.

On the Devil's Dyke
for Michael Vince

In the hedgerows
                along this walk
songbird nests abound; and –
                as my dog runs on
interpreting
                on air and earth

rank traces and warm lingerings that
her cold nose pursues
                    ahead of me –
the birds flutter out and away;
and beasts of undergrowth and hedgerow,
                    rabbit, fox and weasel,
stir within the radius of her scenting
unseen mostly,
                    though from time
to time
                    ahead of us
a red or brown
                    streaks
the crisp white of the chalk ridge, and passes
through the eye's enduring field
                    of green
and brown-and-green
                    bound
in the clasp of the arched blue.
                    There the skylarks
our footfalls drive from the warm clench of
nestling in the grass
                    appear and disappear,
become what is the
                    audible extent –
beyond sight – of the sky

                    *

One might as well
                    be walking further south,
the chalk hills there, it could be
                    the South Downs.
But no:
                    this is a made place, here
in the deep bone and sanctum
                    of the land
is stamped the signature,
                    the *homo fecit*,

of those who dug what we
                  still call
(as the feared Norsemen did)
                  a *dyke* –
no Saxon *ditch* (where a tramp
                  might bed down).

                  *

Defence
                  was what they had in mind who
with this causeway
                  bridged the fen to guard
their landward flank and
                  insulate
a territory
                  plants, birds and beasts
ignore.
                  And though you pass
from time to time
                  into some tangled hedge,
are drawn into –
                  enmeshed in, even –
green of the earth's making,
                  yet you emerge
on the bare ridge-way
                  and across the trench
survey
                  the furrowed ploughland in retreat,
envisage
                  the advance of bristling armies
held
                  in your long watch.

                  *

A spring day
                  and I lie back
on the full flank of the earth,

          the sloped wall of the bulwark.
I am weight, borne by what
          holds me down –
as the larks
          rise, till they are
out of range and
          the blank sky is all
the eye beholds,
          the heart and ear
tugged
          by a lilt and stagger that ascend
beyond perceiving: air
          their scope of territory, their
earthly dwelling.

          Listen!
sing the larks
          down to me: *you,*
a man, live in a place. More,
          in a palimpsest of places:
landscape history creed the word.
Through us you may infer those
          other worlds your map
and composite of places must at best
imply.
          Worlds often glimpsed
beyond your earthworks, ramparts, palisades.

East Anglia

III

The Natural History of the Rook

The rooks are Gothick which have brought to mind
The naturalist Charles Waterton. He wrote
With care and indignation: an explorer:
A solitary who loved, above all creatures,
The birds of the air. When at his burial
A linnet sang out, fact gave rise to legend:
That the flotilla of black barges floating
His body to its lakeside grave had been
Escorted by long flights of birds in mourning.

Among them, rooks. From trees they pinnacle
Like symptoms of a fantasy, their humped
Black shapes unfold now, lifting, taking wing
To drape the sky with signs of lamentation.

No. Waterton – who one phantasmal night
Of gloom and tempest wrote in quietness,
Not fantasy not legend, but 'the history
Of the rook' – in the rook saw no gloom, would not
Submit to the 'blue devils' conjured up
By the November fogs but would combat them
With 'weapons of ornithology'.
                                        He had,
'Having suffered himself and learned mercy',
Laid his guns down, walled in his park and lake,
And made a pause in nature.
                                        There he watched,
Rejoicing in cacophony – explored
Downward
                toward a silence
                                        undisturbed
The barn owl winged its day through,
                                        made a space
Where rooks alighted, their gregarious croak
In tune with an unheard polyphony
His prose, which does not venture to transcribe it,
Bespeaks. Of science and his own estate

He made himself
                a sanctuary
                        the mind
Questing could enter into, haunt in freedom,
And dwell in, freed of its own hauntings.
                                Blithe
You must have been, Charles Waterton, to know
That the inequitable penal laws
Enforced by ignorance and sentiment
Against all 'pests and vermin', now repealed
By you, no longer warped the needful cycles
Of breeding and predation. Blithe you were
From your high perch to watch the darting turquoise
Spear the still pool, to hear the barn owl screech
No special doom to man, and see the rooks
Fly overhead in the dawn light to pass
Into the still remote, unmediated
Variety of inhuman atmosphere.

Near Walsingham

Springs rise where saints have prayed,
                Tradition says;
        And tells of rivulets and wells
                Conceived of rumoured deities.

But streams would have obeyed
                No peremptory hand.
        Where water has already blessed the land
                Saints choose to pray.

Gods walk when glint and spade
                Strike, as it brims,
        A buried watercourse. One dreams
                A cryptic meaning for the source:

Meaning which haunts the shade
        That falls by bridge and ford,
    Lodged in the thought and speech that harken toward
            The interminable

Tale given and not made
            Or understood,
    Which haunts the place. What we might say
        Of what it tells would speak of God.

Home

The lone man harkens to the calm voice,
His expression ajar – as if the draught
On his face were a breath, a friendly breath,
Returning, beyond belief, from time gone by.

The lone man harkens to the ancient voice
His fathers throughout the ages have heard,
Clear and composed, a voice that much like
The green of the pools and hills deepens at evening.

The lone man knows a voice of shadow,
Caressing, and welling forth in the calm tones
Of a secret spring: intently his eyes closed
He drinks it down, and seems not to have it near him.

It is the voice that, one day, halted the father
Of his father, and each of the dead blood.
A woman's voice that whispers in secret
On the threshold of home, at the fall of darkness.

after Cesare Pavese

Homecoming
A Theme and Variations

1. *Mid-Winter*

The year goes out in wrath. And through the winter
Are scattered little days like cottages.
And lampless, hourless nights; and grey mornings,
Their indistinguishable images.

Summertime, autumn – time and season passing,
And brown death has seized on every fruit.
And new cold stars appear now in the darkness,
Unseen before, even from the ship's roof.

Pathless is every life. And every path
Bewildered. The end unknown. And whoso seeks
And finds a path finds that his utterance breaks
Off in sight of it, empty the hands he shakes.

2. *A Winter Evening*

When snow falls on pane and sill,
Long peals are borne on evening air;
The board is laid for many there
In a house provided well.

On their wanderings, several others
Come to the gate by dark ways.
Gold blossoms the tree of grace
Where cool sap in the earth gathers.

The wanderer quietly steps across
A threshold pain has turned to stone.
On the board glow bread and wine
In all the radiance of loss.

3. *A Threshold*

You, centaury, O lesser star,
You birch, you fern, you oak:
Near me you stay as I go far...
Home, into your snare we walk.

Black on a bearded palm tree
Hangs cherry-laurel bunched like grapes.
I love, I hope, I believe...
The small date, split open, gapes.

A saying speaks – to whom? To itself: *Servir*
*Dieu est régner...*I can
Read it, I can – it is coming clear –
Get out of Me-no-unnerstan.

after Georg Heym, 'Mitte des Winters'
Georg Trakl, 'Ein Winterabend'
Paul Celan, 'Kermorvan'

For the Fly-Leaf of a King James Bible

...in dürftiger Zeit
        Hölderlin

Now, in our needy time,
    These words so flush with hope
Probe at the heart that aches toward the past
    For the god not yet come.

Cadence and phrase and tone –
    Derived by Jacobean
Divines from Tyndale and from Coverdale,
    Refined – gain resonance.

A rhythm draws the mind
Through theirs to older scores:
Lollard and Saxon texts; Latin behind,
A plainchant barely heard.

Then Greek, Hebrew, the first
Utterance of the word
Of one the many tongues have, differently,
Called 'God' with the same thirst.

This text – new from the press –
Already smelt of a time
Past, as if left to fust in cellars: earth-
begrimed, already foxed.

Now, in our needy time,
Virtue and beauty seem
In dark, like heady vintage, to mature:
Full-bodied and obscure.

Antiphonal Sonnets
Of John Taverner

I

Suppose a man were dying and this sound
Washed over him: it would not be like sleep
But waking to set eyes for the first time
On the world, ours, yet other. For the sense
Of things would be the things themselves and words
Would gem the melismatic harmony
Rarely, articulating it. The mind –
In a language, the great mass of whose words
Are shattered into vagrant syllables
By gay polyphony – would edge towards
The scope of revelation, which is speechless.

Now, in the place of death, an angel sits
And speaks to three who mourn of interim,
Announces that the second day is done.

II

This was the world: the word.
                              Gratuitous day,
Stained by a red or a blue glaze, confined
By aspiring stone to space with no horizon:
Earthly things that composed an allegory
Which guessed at heaven. He cast given speech
Against the bossed and starry vaults, shattered it
To falling fragments, harmonies – a fertile
Resonance, as much like beauty as like that
It seemed at length to mask: in empty space
A simple disembodied word, the truth.
Then beauty was the hoofbeats in the nave,
The radiant shower of glass, a mace that knocked
Devotion from her pedestal, the flames
That burnt the rood in the broad light of day.

Gothic Polyphony

Space: tall, with no horizon. Plainsong scales
And vines the branched and foliating thrust
Of stone: to bloom polyphony: which fails
Against the ribbed vault's bossed and fretted crust.

To Nicholas Hawksmoor

When, as at Beverley Minster or All Souls,
You ape the Gothic, art is all façade.
Forms moulded of your substance, clear and hard,
Weigh with a Roman virtue. What controls

The impulse, at Christ Church, that would have soared
Through broken cornices to where a spire
Defined not form but anguish and desire,
Becomes your very theme at Castle Howard,

The Mausoleum. Private grief, though lost
In generalities of hope resigned,
There haunts the orders which the patient earth

Sustains for ruin. And something of the north
Troubles your cool sobriety of line
With aspiration and an edge of frost.

Venice

Salt-bleached marble, the green stain of seaweed.

A face the sea dismembers and remembers
Looks back at those who lean towards it, drowning
In admiration, in reflected glory.

Here man hath set his footprint on the waters.
We see the tides disperse it, see them relinquish
The white of marble and the green of seaweed.

A Woodland Scene

We think we detect a date: in the 1860s, is it? – for that would fit. But no, it is merely a calligraphy of shadow and reflection, which leaves (overhanging it) have trailed across the stream in the foreground.

Then the painter's name, Maltby. This, we find, occurs in the standard reference book, but with different initials.

*

Watercolour overlaid with bodycolour. 'Ruskinian' a friend calls it. And so it is: in its anxious piety – in the endeavour to speak, crisply, of the transitory variegations of light on bark, or, where a bough has been shorn off, of light on pith; everywhere modified by the intervention of leaves, translucent or shadow-casting. Ruskinian, too, in the implied continuity of the given world with whatever a mesh of boughs and branches, contained within an arbitrary rectangle, can itself contain. Speaking, then, of the world at large, the picture expounds no painter, is devotional.

Encrusted with light, the leaves lose substance. Fretted with bodycolour, surface becomes depth. It is a sunny day. In our looking, we cool ourselves on the banks of a stream. We are somewhere in the depths of a wood. No people, no birds or beasts, and the world is still.

*

The craftsman who will restore it seems to care as much for frame, mount and glass as for the picture. 'Fine handmade glass, that' – and how can he tell? He holds it horizontal to the eye and, see, light moves in waves across the lucid, tumbling surface, as if engendered by the glass itself. A still, translucent sea – becalmed – of greens and blues. Hung in its frame the glass, like the foliage it reserves for us, both absorbs and reflects, draws in and throws back such light as has entered the room. To the eye of the room-dweller, it interprets the light of the forest.

The frame is of oak. Dull with bituminous varnish and begrimed, until I stripped it with caustic. Then as the water dried, a rose-colour seemed to flush, elusively, in the damp grain of it. We shall preserve what we can of that, and the glass. But the mount has decayed, gone brown. And the card the picture was stuck on is pocked with mould: 'Foxing' says the craftsman – an impurity in the glue can cause it, or a dead fly. All this must be renewed.

*

It used to hang, I remember, in the dullest room of my parents' house, a room usually locked. Later, I rescued it from a windowless box-room. I have hung it near a window now, well in the light.

On occasion the shade of the room blends with the shade of the woodland. Though often, where a tree trunk casts its shadow, daylight falls. Or the pool of imperfect glass becomes opaque with reflections that ripple above inferred profundity. From the other side of the room one begins to see (after long acquaintance) how the picture's uniformity of surface actually appears to tilt inwards, receding into distance through a region of paint where the light's greenish tints are touched with blue.

*

This blue is a threshold, the frame its gate or door. The wood is uninhabited. Let the picture's making and preserving restore to the woodland its absent spirits, recall to the hearthside our household gods.

The Parable of the Sower

Stained glass in the Arts & Crafts style, set in a medieval church

I

The sower goes out to sow. His sense and form
Move only in a landscape of stained glass;
      The leads like ivy stems,
      Enmeshing, bind him in.
Outside, it is afternoon; inside, the sun
Irradiates a face in shadow, eyes
      Inclined toward the earth,
      Crimsoning underfoot.
The glory round about and through his limbs
Is vision in excess of daily need,
      Devotion in the work
      Dispersed beyond the seed.

II

Victorian glass of eighteen ninety-seven,
Replacing the clear light in the west wall
      In homage to a time
      That built as if for ever.
The vision is of a vision that transfigured
Perspectives on the clear field; but with skill
      The craftsman has contained,
      Edged, the unearthly glow.
His observation accurate, the self
A blemish that his labour should efface,
      Devotion to his craft
      Speaks through the pictured face.

III

The sower does not see the field he sows.
He walks in rapture, but his eyes are glazed

With sorrow not his own,
That has no root in earth.
It is the craftsman's sorrow, for he gave
These paradisal colours to the earth
But when he looked on earth
He found an absence there.
Here wayside, thorn, good ground and stony ground
Are stained through with devotion, with his need
For things to mean – the word
Secreted in the seed.

The Peaceable Kingdom
for Tamsin and Gabriel

The wolf also shall dwell with the lamb, and the leopard shall lie down with the kid;
and the calf and the young lion and the fatling together; and a little child shall lead them.

This morning, as I watch my son
    Play with a loved toy horse so small
    He need not fear it, I recall
His elder sister, not yet one,

Behind her cot bars, turning to peep
    At me or, through the orbit of
    The animals that wheeled above
Her head, to watch enlarging sleep

Involve her tiny world – her laugh
    Hushed, and the babble, that addressed
    And answered it. Like things possessed,
Kangaroo, tiger and giraffe,

Pivoted from an elephant's
    Huge bulk, in genial caricature
    Grinning in disregard of her,
Went by her with a nod or prance.

Animals prowling through the air
    In cycles of pursuit, restrained
    From conflict by the space ordained
For harmony of movement: where

Else could the like be found but in
    A mind whose thoughts cannot efface
    With reasoning that longed-for place,
The garden of our origin –

Which she had glimpsed, who thought and saw
    Nothing she could have known, a child
    Looking with trust upon the wild
Through distance unaccounted for?

Could this be that Arcadia,
    Where 'inward laws that ruled the heart'
    Ruled nature, the Creator's art,
As well? Man the Artificer

Then was not: for his work presents,
    Apart from us, a world we stand
    Apart in and would understand;
He frees it from inconsequence,

Showing us, through attention paid
    To things the distances remove,
    That what is feared with reason, love
Need not renounce. Therefore he made

That mobile bestiary whose course
    My girl watched, and these animals
    Cluttered inside their farmyard walls,
Now, by my boy, who lifts a horse

As if he thought to elevate
    The mystery of flesh and blood,
    Priest-like toward an unknown god,
To praise and to propitiate.

Chinoiserie: The Porcelain Garden

Empty, flicked by a fingernail, the bowl
  Rings with the charm of vacancy. A girth
Of pure abstraction binds your world: a whole,
Void of anxiety and fond recall,
                That stands free of the earth.

Revellers in blue glaze, your endless day
  Persuades you there is ground for careless mirth
That does not cloy. Nothing you do or say
Has death in it, as if your primal clay
                Were not derived from earth.

The matter of your converse? Nothing said.
  What profits you, what is your life there worth?
You smile. (Olympian… Mandarin…) The dead,
Even, could not be more disinterested
                Or less ruled by the earth.

On the calm surface of the pool appears,
  Turned on its head, the world that gave you birth,
Denied you growth. And our world is to yours
What you are to the pool, whose rippling clears
                Inconsequence from earth.

There you look on, and we glimpse paradise:
  A dream of beauty and a form of dearth.
One touch of pain, unmimed, might turn to vice
Your virtues. Beauty is gloss. Like constant ice,
                Polar, yet of the earth.

Prayer for my Children

Te lucis ante terminum

Before the end of daylight, Lord
   Dweller in things, we pray you keep
   The custom of your watch when sleep
Annihilates you in our thought.

Untrouble us with dreams; the grim
   Phantasmagoria of the night
   Remove. In sleep the inward sight
Wakes and is powerless to condemn.

And, distant Father, if you hear
   The outcry of a sleeping child,
   Keep soul and body undefiled.
Then, in the absence, you are near.

OF EARTHLY PARADISE

(1992)

TO THE MEMORY OF MY MOTHER
K.S.W. (1904–1985)

Alive, I could not write for you, who dead
Live in the words you planted in my head.

I

Invocation

Unanswering voice,
Sustainer,
Lady or Lord:
I have no choice
But to attend
Your silent word.

I think again
Of the first poet
Of my tongue:
Abandoning
The sweet, profane
Intoxication
Of plucked string
And exploit sung.

At your command
He sang creation.

He had withdrawn
To where
His silence was:
Where cattle stand
And, sleeping, moan,
Stamp, grumble, snort.

As in high places dawn
Will spring
Sudden from stone,
So from the dung
And bed-straw rose
His made thought.

Angel or Muse,
Because I do
Not hear your voice
Yet cannot choose
But speak, I pray

Let my words be
Such that they grow
From my silence
Answering you,
As they
Must answer me.

Three Brueghel Paintings

I

This is the world (the painter says)
Reduced by ice and snow, bone-bare.
    Then ride in mercenaries.
Armed to the teeth they introduce
    Fear, panic and despair.
They'd trace a king. How can they know
        He is not here?

II

Where earth encounters heaven, cloud
Frays on the trees that spike the air.
    Ranks crumble to a crowd
Of stragglers. Some, bemused and dazed
    By light's intrusion, stare
At one the light has felled, who sees
        What is not there.

III

No myth informs this wintry view
Enhanced by no nostalgic care
    For skies of southern blue.
Skaters delight in circumstance
    Three hunters come to share
Who slant against winds charged with snow
        From who knows where.

The Massacre of the Innocents
The Conversion of St Paul
Hunters in the Snow

St Francis Preaching to the Birds
for Tamsin

Not angels these; although
Their melody and flight
Subsume the world, their wings
Substantiating light.

This man whom inwardness
And gracious thought have blessed,
Possessing nothing, knows
Both ear and eye possessed.

Their being crowds against
His gates of sense: to move
Into the mind, where language
Declares the movement love,

Though love is his, not theirs.
They, living beyond reach,
Indifferent to meaning,
Are made anew in speech.

The San Damiano Crucifix

which spoke to St Francis

A church about to fall.
The saint of poverty
Knelt in the church to pray,
Loving its poverty.

Flesh-tint and gold leaf
Hung there above him: a cross.
With bodily ears he heard
A voice speak from the cross

In pain, exhorting him
Repair my broken house.
Stone by stone he repaired
The body of that house:

For though the letter kills,
The spirit and the word
Move in the flesh alone.
So too, although the words

Spoken by painted wood
And answered in his work
May not be what we hear,
It is a speaking work.

The Coat of Many Colours

Do not interpretations belong to God?

Joseph:

Rich colour signifies deep inwardness.
The bending sheaves, the sun's, the moon's decline
Are colours in this coat, my father's gift.

Some bleed and blend. Others, like potentates,
Stand out – see! – urgent and peremptory.

One of the brothers:

All his tall stories, dreams he calls them, stress
His own pre-eminence, its outward sign
That coat he swaggers in ... What but that gift
Has he to show? ... How his pretension grates,
The smugness posing as authority!

Potiphar's wife:

My mordant lust, no matter what he says,
He woke in me. Now I dream his body's line,
Its nervous thrust imprisoned, and the gift
Of so reading desire his eye translates –
Through cold reflection – heat to chastity.

Pharaoh:

Amun, we are all, gaudy or poor our dress,
Rich with an inwardness that seals us thine!
I raise this man to greatness for a gift
Beyond such wealth, since what his night creates
His day interprets with lucidity.

Jacob:

I dreamt you had not gone, though dreamt it less
The nearer death I grew. O son of mine,
Now I have found you, death shall be a gift,
And dream and understanding the twin gates
I pass through as I near reality.

Cattle Market
for Gabriel

Why brook'st thou, ignorant horse, subjection?
Why dost thou, bull and boar, so seelily
Dissemble weakness, and by one man's stroke die,
Whose whole kind you might swallow and feed upon?
Donne

Seely or silly?
               Timorous beasts
Thwacked and buffeted into pens
Clamour against the world, although
The hands they suffer at are men's.
Terror masters them – it protests,
Seems to resist, then lets them go

Lambs to the slaughter, pigs, cows…
Men who stand and look on equate
Value with fleshly substance – price
The measure of it; and this they state
By way of nods and puckering brows.
Yet the whole place seems paradise

To one of them, who does not count
Or bid, through whom a passion stares
And feeds on what he cannot grasp:
Each penned or passing creature wears,
For him, an auric splendour, faint
But clear and there. His fingers clasp

A hand above him, trembling at
The power a solicitous father bends
To shield him from. But through the boy's
Passion – uncertain where it tends,
What it might mean – the man has caught
Something of brilliance, so that he toys

With likenesses, which grope and guess
At meaning: through such wintry light
As lingers in the frosted breath
Looping these mindless skulls, one might
(He fancies) look on blessedness.
What moves him, though, beyond all myth,

Is what the bidders, were they to break
Silence, might judge beneath contempt –
The vacant, dumb docility
With which most other lives are stamped.
This powerlessness to choose or speak
So fleshes out the verb *to be*

That children innocent of pain
Take it for glory: which, absurd
To traders who provide for them,
Seems emblem of a fate endured
To those who dream of angels on
The darkened hills of Bethlehem.

Christmas Eve, 1983

Birdsong and Polyphony

The birds in this illuminated manuscript –
Wood-dove and song-thrush, chaffinch and goldfinch –
Are radiant marginalia that gloss
The notion of music, the notation of music.

We take it that their natural artifice
Would drench creation in polyphony;
They perch at the white borders of the page,
The score behind them, held back from flight.

The Infinite Variety

1. *The Museum of Natural History, Santa Barbara*
for Edgar Bowers

All the birds of the region in one room,
Condor to humming-bird! Only a glance takes in
Pelican, golden eagle, blue-jay, wren…
Two hundred maybe, stuffed, posed, poised for flight.
What need (you say) has nature for so many
Exquisite variations? She selects
Each kind, are we to think, by fine distinction –
In the whole country, say, some forty species
Of warbler, each a different intersection
Of colour, music, mass, texture and form?
Or was it some such randomness as jars
Through the San Andreas Fault, which will in time
Shatter this state of high prosperity
To nameless this and that: did some such flaw
Cause these named rifts, that branch in plenitude?

2. *Minerals from the Collection of John Ruskin*

The boy geologist who clove the rocks
Here on display grew up to be the great
Philosopher of colour into form
And, in the products of just workmanship,
Discerned the paradigm of the just state.

It was the Lord's design he made apparent –
These bands and blocks of azure, umber, gilt,
Set in their flexing contours, solid flow
That had composed itself in its own frame:
Red garnet neighbouring mica, silver white;
A slice of agate like an inland sea…

In manhood, similarly, his eye judged how
Good stone splits fairly at the mason's touch;
How painters stay their colour, shape the run
And blotch of it to images of truth.
He taught that these, and others like them, might
– Workers with hand or mind – be driven less
By harsh need or harsh fate than by the call
Imagination hears to make new worlds:
Which honour in epitome this world,
Ruled by its fluid and elusive forms.

If chance be providential, the taught eyes
Of those who paint or carve so should instruct us
In justice and original design.

3. *My Father's Collection of Indian Butterflies and Moths*
for Val

I have no names for them, foreign to me,
Although my father named and numbered each.
Nor, now they are gone, can I recall
One individual insect – neither shape
Nor colour nor composition. So I brood
On formless memories of moths so big
They looked like two splayed hands linked at the thumbs,
And butterflies arranged by deviation
From an unstated norm of their design:
You could imagine them – they were so vibrant –
Cut from some miniature of Shah Jahan's.

I was three when my father died; my mother
Outlived him forty years. When she died too,
My sister and I brought down the insect boxes –
Perhaps in expectation that that vision
Of plenitude, long stowed, awaited us.
I could not breathe to think of them. We opened
To nothing but a hint of dust, and pins

Staked upright, row on row, like monuments
To that which he had left us, though it felt
As if what he had left us had not been.

The Thirst

A kingfisher darting the green scum on a pool
Leaves it unbroken. Out of and over long grass
An erratic career, and a hare has become distance.

These things should be enough. But the old Adam
In me calls for their naming, seeing in them
Not at all more than their being there, but more
Than that they are. The one lust we can never
Wholly contain. The one unquenchable thirst.

The body barely withdrawn from the spring of delight,
And a full silence. Unbroached it cannot be.

To Robert Wells
on his translation of 'The Georgics'

This is your poem of fields and flocks and trees
(As it was Virgil's) for the words are yours,
If words are of a poet, which are ours
And not ours either but the names of things.

II

A Catalogue of Flowers

Wild Flowers

Ragwort and mallow, toadflax and willow-herb
Trick out the waste-ground patchwork that I thread
To no end, not for delight, but with a passion
Such as they feel who are obsessed with death –

Though this is not death. I linger here
Where rot assumes these terrace-house cadavers,
And brick-rubble, riven paving-slabs, puddled ruts
Are cordoned off by bindweed tapestries

On looms of fence-wire. One might think neglect
Cultivates that for which it has made way –
The minor glories idleness in passing
Names 'wallflower', 'dog rose', maybe 'traveller's joy'.

Bindweed Song

I am convolvulus.
I prosper where your ways are undermined
By war or social lapse. So call me weed:
Bindweed that comes uncalled for, weeds that bind.

Where eyesores are I flourish –
Where mildew, rat and spider occupy
Your seat and artefact. They are the world,
You the ephemerids, and what am I

Who have wound a way back in,
Who mesh and drape – until they all cohere –
Hedge, pathway and door-frame? See, passer-by,
How beauty decks the substance of your fear.

An Autumn Vision

In dreams, in bombed-out houses,
  Where childhood used to play,
  Among brambles and briar roses
And grass running to seed I pick my way,

  Until I reach a clearing
  Of strafed and harrowed ground
  Where tombs founder, smoke blackened,
Corroded angels mourning, and no sound.

  Finding the grave – a broadsword
  Laid on memorial loam
  As the tomb cross – and leaning forward
To gouge the sooty lichen from a name,

  I glimpse beyond in the greenwood
  Some purple artifice
  (A helmet plume?) flourishing over
The drawn, despairing, honourable face

  Of one whose quest advances
  Down broken paths that tend
  Toward a past locked in battle
With wrong he knows no future can amend.

Post-war Childhoods
for Takeshi Kusafuka

If there were no affliction in this world we might think we were in paradise.
          Simone Weil, *Gravity and Grace*

You, born in Tokyo
In nineteen forty-four,
Knew the simplicity
Occasioned by a war.
In London it was so,
Even in victory –
In defeat, how much more.

Knew it I say – and yet,
Born to it, you and I,
How could we in truth have known?
It was the world. You try
To make articulate,
In language not your own,
What it was like and why.

Nature returned (you say)
To downtown Tokyo –
In your voice, some irony
Defending your need to go
That far: what other way
Of like economy
Is there of saying so?

Your images declare
The substance of the phrase:
Bomb craters, urban grass,
A slowworm flexing the gaze
Of the boy crouching there;
Moths, splayed on the glass,
Like hands lifted in praise.

A future might have drawn
On what such things could tell.
You heard, even as you woke,
Accustomed birdsong fill
The unpolluted dawn,
Heard a toad blurt and croak
In some abandoned well.

They call it desolation,
The bare but fertile plot
You have been speaking of.
You grew there, who have taught
Me much of the relation
Affliction bears to love
In Simone Weil's scoured thought.

I, too, have images.
A photograph: St Paul's,
The dome a helmeted head
Uplifted, as terror falls.
The place I knew, not this
But a city back from the dead,
Grew fireweed within walls.

I played over dead bombs
In suburban villas, a wrecked
Street of them where, run wild,
Fat rhododendrons cracked
The floors of derelict rooms:
It seemed to a small child
An Eden of neglect.

If we two share a desire,
It is not that either place,
Still less the time, should return.
If gravity and grace
Survive a world on fire
Fixed in the mind, they burn
For things to be in peace.

Conservancy
for Heather Glen

It was the treatment of the banks by the Thames Conservancy Board, which regularly cut down all the flowers and cleared the stream of its pleasant flowering reeds and rushes, which so enraged Morris.

Philip Henderson, *William Morris*

'These were the buds that tipped desire
And shaped what might be from what is.
Now summer grants the river's edge
This wealth of colour: bulrushes,

Long purples, a strong yellow flower
That's close and buttony, horse mint,
Mouse ear, belated meadow-sweet,
And dark blue mug-wort – not a hint

Of luxury in the excess
That freshens in the passing gust,
Or anarchy in the design
Of that which grows where grow it must.

Yet now the Thames Conservancy,
Subversive of the perfect state,
Instructs the servile ministers
Of order to annihilate

These frail entanglements, this fine
Community of loveliness,
Where natural harmony, though not
Traceable, governs none the less.

I loose my anger, then withdraw
To dream the paradise within:
Rich banks of colour that declare
Proudly a humble origin

Without – I weave them from the dark
And so, approximately, chart
The paradise we share, whose stream
Rises and rises in the heart.'

Alkanet
for Di

I'd seen it before but had not heard it named:
The leaves like nettles, a blue flower that peers
Above dustbins and detritus. Called alkanet,
It's a kind of wild borage, the book says.

A year, more or less, since we moved in.
That long June evening, you having gone back
To the old house, I stayed on sanding the floor
Until I could no longer see to work,

Then for the first time left by the back way.
Anxiety dulled by labour, conscious alone
Of sweat and dust and my limbs' weight, I felt
The quiet that is exhaustion coming on

And in the alley, among dark shapes of leaf –
Palpable shadows that I waded through,
My hands tingling – saw tiny flowers that retained
The sky's late intensity of blue.

When I got home I told you of the flowers
And of the light I'd seen them in. Since then
I know you have often thought of them as mine,
Not seeing that I cared for them as yours.

To Paint a Salt Marsh

Samphire and mare's tail and the salt marsh.

Nothing appears to have movement here
but the birds – it is where the white tern
pivots his swift course and on the tideline
dunlin and sandpiper dibble.
                            Otherwise,
at low tide, it's as if the brown sea
clogged in the mudflats. A spar,
tall and near the vertical, splits the view.

And on the horizon a grass-thatched sand-dune
looms like a northern fell. It
lays on the water's stillness precisely
its own stillness.

III

In the sweat of thy face shalt thou eat bread,
till thou return unto the ground.

Work
for Donald Davie, sculptor in verse

1

Adam,
in the sweat of his brow,
ate bread.

Eve, in pain,
laboured
to bear fruit.

She spun, she wove…
Adam carved:

not that the stones
be made bread,
but rather

that – stone worked
and habitation
hewn from it –

bread be eaten,
fruit borne.

2

At the point of the chisel
what was
a block of stone
a corbel, a capital
becomes
pierced with darkness
a leafy glade
              of the forest
brought indoors

And beneath it, cut
from the general view
for God
for the swineherd your brother –
– where an acorn-cup, empty
tells of the forest floor –
two pigs
        two snouts rather
rooting among leaves

3

A mullion –
cleft and branching, then
in the marble
cut leafage, un-
furling
      clear of it

Such needless beauty
the Protestant work ethic
has no time for

Though it was hand
and labour first
bowed the mason
to the task

Which issues in this praise
of the maker of leaves and stone

The Law of the House

A house of good stone
cut fair and square,
Justice the governor –

spotless, abstract,
a goddess held in common
by all people. And all

particulars too, by virtue
of being, acknowledge
her true sway. As economy

is house law, it follows
that builders should dispose
with precision – that is,

lapidary justice.
It is a scene in fresco –
equable rule

there, figured
by impartial light
and clear space. But if

the contrasted masses
move, clash, if the ground quake
and dislodge stone,

if storm
set person against
person or against thing,

what syntax in confusion
can piece together
the logic of her dark will?

At the Grave of Ezra Pound
San Michele, Venice

1

here lies a man
of words, who in time
came to doubt their meanings

who therefore confines
himself to two words
only here

EZRA POVND

minimal
the injury done
to the white stone

none
to the earth
it rests upon

2

The spoils of a corsair –
who ranged the Mediterranean
and brought home
porphyry, alabaster, lapis lazuli
and every hue and current of veined marble.

In the bayleaves' shade
dumb now
and within earshot
of the stilled Adriatic
deaf, rests
under white marble
la spoglia, the remains.

At the Grave of William Morris
Kelmscot Churchyard

1

where you lie
      northman
your grey gable
rugg'd with lichen

roof raised above
      no walls,
soul's shelter
from the sky's bluster,

and there underneath it
      rests
that restless body
rootless among roots

2

Through the mouth and nostrils
sprouts greenery

or rime glitters
in the great beard

Desire

like ivy on a gravestone
binds him to this one place

like grass threading
the bluebells and the cowslips
braids him into it –

this holy place,
made holier by
his love of it

by his love

Fonte Branda in Siena

Fonte Branda, wrote Ruskin, *I last saw*
under the same arches where Dante saw it.
He drank of it then
                    and every time the near
pentameters of his prose recur to me,
I too see the place again:

the *loggia* of red brick, in white stone
the jutting bestial heads
                    and within,
shade and the still pool.

Whenever the Englishman went there he would find
rage at injustice,
true words that pinion falsehood and cupidity,
bitterness in the sweet spring, the hiss
of white hot metal plunged in the cool water
as he drank.
            I think of that sad face,
the charred brain behind it, the word flow.
And in my thought, as if toward the calm
of memory, he stoops to drink.
And every time he stoops the Florentine
in his pink coat, not crowned with laurel yet,
moves into range
                    much as another's words
return to the quiet mind.

They do not see me there. But the place-names
hold them in view — *Siena, Fonte Branda* —
by brimming water, on the point of speech.

Ruskin, Praeterita III, 4, §86
Dante, Inferno, xxx, 49–90

A Plaque
Pensione Calcina, Venice

In this house lived   in 1877

JOHN RUSKIN

High-priest of art
in the stones of Venice   in her St Mark's
in almost every monument in Italy
he sought   at one and the same time
the craftsman's soul and the soul of the craftsman's people.

Every block of marble, bronze-casting and canvas
every thing proclaimed aloud to this man's senses
that beauty is religion
if human virtue sustain it
and a reverent people acknowledge it.

The Commune of Venice   in recognition
XXVI January MDCCCC

From the Italian

To a Poet from Eastern Europe, 1988

Strong drink –
>   on the bare table a neat vodka,
Innocently transparent as pure water,
Shimmers before you, with your fence of bone
(Stake shoulders, propping arms) set up around it,
>   As if, out there alone,
The spirit needed body to defend it.

From where I stand, though, I can count the cost
(The soured breath, sickly flush and hollow chest)
You pay, at forty-five, for what you savour.
It fortifies, calms the stomach, and yet still
>   – Alas! greybeard cadaver –
Consumes the body as pure spirit will.

Consider, as you waste, how we are stewards
Of our bodies, yes, yet strangely how you thrive
On the sick body politic your words
Bite into as you're bitten: how your thirst
>   For truth keeps you alive,
Writhing in anger, choking on disgust.

To Haydn and Mozart

You were both endowed with flair and with, no doubt,
What is called genius; but I think of you
Bent over your claviers, two men at work,
Fending off discord with your fingertips.
At work you could stay unmoved by what you knew
Of exploitation or of penury,
Uncomprehending ignorance and pride,
Loss, disappointment, pain. You turned from these
To forms that would not warp with labour, for
You heard in them the possibility
Of grace, which echoes order in the mind.

The Kitchen Table
in memory of my mother

Making a home was
what you could do
best; and cookery

(the ritual at
the heart of it) you had
a kind of genius for.

So what I first
recall, thinking of you,
is a creamy table-top,

the grain etched
crude and deep, the legs
stained black, and you

at work, with rolling-pin
or chopping-board or
bowl; then, later,

presiding over
guests or children at each
day's informal feast.

Your homeliness
displaced now, what survives
for me of it

is this: which
now becomes a model
of true art:

bare boards scrubbed clean,
black, white,
good work as grace, such

purity of heart.

IV

Charon's Bark

to my mother

1

It's the being left behind
I can't believe:
me stranded on this shore
and glimpsing you,
too far out, too baffled by the crowd
of they might be twittering shoppers,
to notice that I stay.

I recognise you by
a look of panic, so faint
who else in the world would notice it,
as you stare back at the shore,
your set eyes blind to the same look
in these that reach out after you.

2

On nights like this
when with snow piled deep it is
too cold to snow any more
in the bitter wind,
I can't get the thought of you out of my mind.

What I keep thinking of
is waking too early on a bright morning
and running to your bed, and jumping in.

On nights like this,
I can't keep the tears back
at the thought of you –
out there in the dark, the snow your coverlet,
unwakably asleep.

Two Journals

I keep two journals. In the first one there's
A record of dreams, fantasies and fears
That edge me toward that commonplace, the Brink:
My evidence, that is, for beak or shrink.

On odd days in the second – now more odd,
Alas, than ordinary – I brood on God,
The distant prospect of his love, and bend
Aesthetics and poetics to that end.

Sadly, I can't conflate them in one text.
There I am crazed, erratic, oversexed,
Here pure, serene and earnest in my quest;
An angel here, there a tormented beast!

So when I write in one, I overlook
Evidence set down in the other book.
So they, between the two of them, divide
The single mind where single truths reside.

The Temple of Aphrodite

1

I woke to nobody. Desire. Intent.
And her to follow as embodiment.

2

Twilight. The streets invite me. They run down
Towards the harbour. In the heart of town

Some common land where road and quayside merge.
A kestrel weighs above. On a grass verge

A rabbit, tempted out, soon bobs away.
I drift back to the shopfronts. Now the day

Is switched off, starker lights illumine whores
Who, between open street and shuttered doors,

Poise, whispering incitements. Manliness,
Withdrawn and shy, rises to the caress

Of smooth obscenity, that heady charm,
Which leads me, not to pleasure nor to harm,

But down an inward subway, a deep maze
Of infinitely bifurcating ways.

3

I meet you in a room too dark for shame
And call you Love, who have no other name.

4

Naked, it feels as if some filmy dress
Still clung invisibly to her bare flesh.

It is like language clothed in irony:
Her body – smooth, particular and free –

Is offered in the name of love, might seem
The incarnation of a general dream;

Yet, though I tremble at her skilled caress,
I know I am not the object of address.

5

What you find – making love, with no love meant –
Is contact without cóntent; without contént.

6

An hour before my train. Leaving the car,
I cross the station to a burger bar

That looks out on the street. I sit and read –
Drink tea, drink good strong prose, and do not heed

The garish colours round me or outside
The urgent traffic at its fullest tide.

Combatively my book affirms the good
Of this world's substance – always understood,

First, that the mind which loves the world is more
Than what it loves; then (in a sense the core

Of such love) that if earthly powers deny
Our love its freedom, we are free to die.

Oh but it's dark already. Across the way
She stands, under a streetlamp, on display,

A handsome woman, black, in red high heels;
A string vest of the selfsame red reveals,

More than it clothes, her breasts' full luxury,
And skin-tight silver ski-pants generously

Outline her other curves, from hip to calf.
I rise, contemplative, then stand and laugh

In the doorway. Words gone, the train can go.
What else in the wide world could move me so?

Amores

I call this latest book Adversity.
Though it is mine, it is obscure to me.
Some passages of love, though, seem more clear
In a dark context, and I gloss them here.

*

It was not quite the last time. Yet, that day,
Orgasm shook my body with a cry
That echoed through me like a long goodbye.
We parted; then you wept, and turned away.

*

We first met maybe seven years ago
But barely more than chatted before this.
Three afternoons of love, and you must go.
I miss you, scarcely knowing whom I miss.

*

Those brieze-block walls: bare in my memory
The room is – basin, bed, one lamp, one chair.
Yet, entering it, I found you also bare,
And lay down in the lap of luxury.

*

Strange that of all things I recall this fact:
Neither the surge of passion nor the act,
But falling asleep like a child no terrors shake,
Who can, because the woman stays awake.

*

Despising though desiring you, I let
Our next date pass, deciding to forget.
I'd known you, say, five hours in fewer days;
Twenty years later, how you touched me stays.

                    *

I see a broken city in your head
(Beautiful lady) ravaged by cross-fire.
But here, against that backdrop, you are led
By civil urgencies of sweet desire.

                    *

You speak of hope and liberty, new love.
Why must I speak of loyalty and despair?
Freedom is our two bodies as they move
And hopelessness the passion we must share.

                    *

I thought myself unscathed, so did not yield,
But ran, till looking back from a safe height,
I saw wrenched bodies on a battlefield
That once had seemed a garden of delight.

                    *

Dear child, dear lady, bless you where you sleep
Alone, who should be sleeping here with me.
My one desire's that your desire should keep
On beating at the gates of reverie.

Re-reading my Poem 'Saxon Buckle'

My amulet against the shocks of time!
I made it twenty years ago and still
Despair and terror, snared in the taut rhyme,
Are held by that old exercise of skill.

I trawled for meaning in the world out there
From then till now. The changing world's changed me.
And still, through emptiness, my words declare:
'Meaning is ours: in this space you are free.'

Transference
for Graham Davies

A moving tableau, so to speak.
On the same couch, week after week,
Talking of absence, I can see
Its likeness bearing down on me:
The ceiling blankness. But if I
Let my glance fall to where the sky
Through the broad window hangs behind
The web of garden life, I find
Love I'd thought dead diffused among
Bright songbirds; they with inhuman song
And vivid colour, as they feed
At the bird table, hit my need
For harmony. And then your voice
Behind me, beyond reach of choice,
Speaks out of darkness and dismay.
De profundis, Domine.

The Dream

Under those heads, an argument of coils,
Protean, polymorphous, serpentine.
Hot breath, bared teeth: the questioning is mine,
The questions not. I strike. A neck recoils,

Gives way before my answer. Thus I hack
Into the bloated flesh of it: thus, thus.
Winged helmet, carven shield: the fabulous
Purity, grace and swiftness of attack!

And still the heads. Day breaks. And no respite.
The questions, now I flag, metamorphose,
The asker changes, then the monster goes,

And still the coils are there, a wraith in light.
I rise, I dress for work; blunt sword, cracked shield.
No more than whisper and the worm's revealed.

In the Greenwood

When Michael Ryan in that forest glade
(Armed and flak-jacketed, his camouflage
Not disentangled quite from leafy shade)
Let out the first spurt of his huge discharge,

He invoked Emptiness: in these dull days
Prince of this land and Regent (for the King
Must brood in exile on our ancient ways
And the green woods of their meandering).

Now, as the echoes die, I hear a man
My countrymen once dreamt of wind his horn –
A note of warning from a vanished wood;

He, gentle yet pugnacious, jovial
And stubbornly enduring, gave up all
His right and fortune to the common good.

1988

The Garden

Efface complexity, forget the bond
Of old affection, trust, ennui… For love,
This room's the world: which all the world beyond,
Although enriched by it, knows nothing of.

Your body is the garden at its heart –
Sweetness and pungency; earth in this place
Is damp, springy with moss, and when I part
The leaves up there, fruit dangles in my face.

Such innocence! But, now you stretch and yawn
And rise, you turn away from me toward
The somewhere-else that is to be endured.
The world is all before us. We shall meet
A messenger with news of our deceit
Where pale flowers shred and tangle on the thorn.

Oasis

The terms of the analogy are strained –
And that is as it should be, for the world
Is nothing but the world and things are called
By names they cannot answer to. Constrained
By what I am to name things, when I see
How beauty proper to a watered place
Extends beyond it to this wilderness,
I call this paradise, which it can't be.

And it is paradise I think of too
When your cool body's fluency and grace
Come near, and nearer, in this desert place
As if the Lord were beckoning through you –
    Though God is darkest when his creatures bless
    And paradise is of the wilderness.

The Earth Rising

The men who first set foot on the bleached waste
That is the moon saw rising near in space
A planetary oasis that surpassed
The homesick longings of our voyaging race:

Emerald and ultramarine through a white haze
Like a torn veil – as if no sand or dust
Or stain of spilt blood or invading rust
Corrupted it with reds, browns, yellows, greys.

So visionaries have seen it: to design
Transparent, luminous and, as if new-made,
Cut from surrounding darkness. Praise the Lord,
For *Heaven and earth* (the psalmist sang) *are thine;*
The foundation of the round world thou hast laid,
And all that therein is. And plague and sword.

V

Caedmon of Whitby
A Libretto

The Hymn

> Nū scylun hergan hefaenrīcaes Uard,
> Metudæs maecti end his mōdgidanc,
> uerc Uuldurfadur, suē hē uundra gihuaes
> ēci Dryctin, ōr āstelidæ.
> Hē āērist scōp aelda barnum
> heben til hrofe, hāleg Scepen.
> Thā middungeard moncynnæs Uard,
> ēci Dryctin, æfter tīadæ
> fīrum foldu Frēa allmectig.

Recitative

There was in the monastery of Whitby a lay brother blessed by God with the gift of song. Indeed, so sweet were his songs that greatly they would inflame the hearts of his hearers, and no other maker could match his cunning. For he learned the art of singing without human instruction, receiving it freely as a gift from God.

Now, although this man dwelt in the monastery many years until he was well stricken in age, he had at no time learned any songs. And sometimes at table, when the company was set to be merry and had agreed that all should sing, each in his turn, he, when he saw the harp to be coming near him, would rise up before supper was done and go out into the night.

One evening, leaving the feasting-hall in this way, he had gone out to the stable of the beasts, which was to be his care for that whole night. And there, at the fitting hour, he had bestowed his limbs to rest, when suddenly he was aware of one standing before him, who addressed him thus:

Aria (The Stranger)

> Caedmon, God speed!
> Why do you turn aside from your great need?
> Why do you stay chaste?
> It is not silent plenty but sad waste.
> Old man already: when will you begin?
> Now, I command you, take up your harp and sing!

Dialogue

Caedmon:

I *cannot* sing. Therefore I left the company in the hall – because I do not know how.

Stranger:

I tell you you must sing to me. Consider no further in your head, but sing as the birds sing.

Caedmon:

I have no matter. What *words* should I sing, even if there were music in my soul?

Stranger:

Sing the beginning of the world: how God made it and the fair creatures that dwell in it.

Aria (Caedmon)

> What holds me back,
> A swimmer,
> On the shore?
> Would the cold shock
> Be more
> Than flesh could bear?

Unanswering voice,
Sustainer,
Mighty Lord:
My tuneless speech
Awaits
Your speechless word.

Recitative

So Caedmon began at once to sing, in praise of God, verses which he had never heard before – and sweet was the sound of them. Then his visitor departed from him, and he awoke, and it was day. But sounding yet in his heart was that very song he had sung before in his sleep. And he went at once to beg audience of the Abbess, and sang the song to her.

The Hymn

Now should we hail   heaven's guardian,
Praise the Maker,   his might and thought,
The Father of glory,   his work: for he gave
To all wonders   one beginning –
        Everlasting Lord.
First he raised   a roof which is heaven
For the sons of men,   *sanctus artifex*;
And then in time,   everlasting Lord,
Mankind's guardian,   he made earth,
Made and adorned it,   almighty King.

KING ALFRED'S BOOK
& OTHER POEMS
(1992–2000)

TO TAMSIN AND GABRIEL

We love best what is given us: no choices
Speak to us like our new-born babies' voices.

Children, if you have ever felt neglected,
Don't blame me. Blame the children I've selected.

On my 'Selected Poems'
1995

I

King Alfred's Book

A King made me. Alfred turned
Roman letters into English speech.
Now, as you read me,
Hear his voice and your mother-tongue
Telling the Roman's tale.

First you must hear: men once loved learning.
The word-hoards they harboured
Were great wealth to them, and solace –
Their books, jewelled and enamelled, richly gilded.
That time is gone.
You see their tracks but you cannot trace them.

Do not allow my unregarded leaves
To flutter in the wind and rain.
These lines of script are ways through the forest.
You, as you read me,
Keep the ways open.

Lindisfarne Sacked

The dragon prows. Dragons' tongues
        flare at the darkness:
                illumination.

House-martin
for M.L.

– like the heart's arrow,
        unerringly home
                to her nest in the ribbed vault.

The River in Springtime

The river seems alive:
    silvery beercans
battening on fat fronds.

The Manor House

'Ramshackle loveliness' was the phrase I wrote,
then cancelled and kept free for use elsewhere:
    the whole feel of the place – as much
        the countryside as his house –

is in that sense of unachieved perfection
and slight neglect that makes for beauty. It might be
    the receding lip of a stone step
        foot-worn to a wave,

or a tie-beam, the curved thew of a bough
black with pitch, or the way each block of stone
    (crudely dressed, set on the soil
        it was dug from time out of mind)

fits so closely yet roughly against stone.
I come outside and imagine him living there,
    as the wind heaves and the loaded tree
        lurches, towards the wall,

its freight of apples. In there, he draws or writes
and apple and grey stone are in his work
    as leaves and feathers are, which seem
        (ruffled in draught, the dust

blown from their pores) fresh from creation. What
is this I feel but love for the man he was
    or must have been? The river willows
        tense hard against the wind

as I drive by a rutted track for the M4:
it is only five miles off and yet (with the river,
 clear as its source, flowing between)
 might as well be a thousand.

Anthem

Suppose him to be a person
whose whole faith is in words,
yet at weekday evensong
 a devout attender,

loving the stained demise
of daylight, as it transfigures
the Gothic walls' pale stone
 with watercolour

and the silhouetted wings
spread in the rafters, resounding
to the voices of boys, their poly-
 phonic ascent.

Then consider him to have heard
an anthem one day, the text
being several lines perhaps
 of his own writing

set to such notes as thwart
the sadness at day's end
with glory (as it were)
 oh *in excelsis*

by a friend to whom a composed
harmony is for the soul
the one lodging, brief but secure,
 on its brief journey.

Psalm

Here the waters converge and in their fork
    we sit on the ground and weep.
        So this is exile.

Their currents flow by me. Why should they heed
    a man in love with the past
        of his own country,

lost to him now, elsewhere? Our home river,
    gone underground, flows counter.
        And when our masters –

half in mockery, yet half curious
    to hear such foreign lore –
        call for an old song,

I hang my harp high on a willow bough
    leaning across the flood.
        Jerusalem,

let the hand that writes these verses wither and die
    if I forget you now
        in this ill time;

let my tongue stick in my throat if I sell short
    the source of all my words,
        fail to remember

where my joys began. In the mean time,
    Daughter of Babylon, you
        have humbled us:

you may publish us to the world, you may ignore us.
    But we have time. In time
        we will be revenged.

Psalm 137

Grace

When you spoke, after dinner,
of haymaking, of loading
the tractor at dusk and the
new fragrance of hay you breathed
in with delight (and so out

in your talk), first came to mind
my garden – the basil there
that stains my fingers with its
pungency, and washed linen
freshening on the line – and then,

on my way home, the prayer you
said before food, which again
now fills me with thanks, as if
savour or scent were the thought
no gift can be good without.

The Pig Man

Carmine Ferretti, aged 69, emerges from the pigsty where he was kept for sixty years by his family. Mr Ferretti, mute and mentally retarded since childhood, had a disability pension, which the family shared.

Newspaper caption

The cameras flash and he lurches into light.
His feet clog in ordure. At sixty-nine,
He has long outlived the companions of his youth.

Look at him. The face is a scared face:
The brain behind it knows, that is to say,
No more than the world in which he finds himself.

His eyes seem to look out from the sides of his head.
They appear to focus on nothing. Head down,
He shambles forward as if led by the nose.

What is more human than a mind deranged?
Here is a mind that is innocent of thought.
What is man, that thou are mindful of him?

Thou hast made him a little lower than the angels
To crown him with glory and worship
And given him dominion over the beasts.

What is a man who knows no other warmth
Than the coarse and steaming flanks of a mother sow,
Our brother in the house of Brother Pig?

The policeman watching over him looks away.
He is sober and expressionless, on duty.
One can tell that he is mindful.

Kaspar Hauser

Who wanted to be a horseman
Who wanted to be what his father had been before him

Who had no father, who had no mother
Who could not ride
Who sprang fully-formed from nowhere

Who knew the floor of a stable
better than he knew the world or knew himself
Who could not tell who had fed him or sustained him

Who lacked speech
Who could not put into words
where he had come from or what was to be his end
Who could not describe the world
Who could not define it

On whom the sins of the fathers were visited
Who was innocent, who was fallen
Who now was to eat bread in the sweat of his face

Who was sub-normal, moronic, mentally disabled,
an inspired visionary, a wolf-boy, a child of God

Who had quickened in his mother's womb
to be flung wailing into the world
Who had fallen from nowhere
and found himself nowhere

Who could not say who had killed him
or why he had had to die

II
Three Epistles

To Thom Gunn, on his Sixtieth Birthday

You won't recall them now – 'The Burial Mound',
'Valhalla', 'The Dead Warrior' – poems which sound
Too much like half-cooked, over-seasoned stews
Of tough ingredients culled from Gunn and Hughes
('Thistles', 'The Byrnies', 'The Warriors of the North',
'The Wound'). Hard man, you read my pourings-forth,
Gauche as they were, with such strict tolerance,
Such courtesy, you never looked askance
At what, derived from you, partook of truth
Though twisted through the fantasies of youth;
You taught me form, reminding me of sense
When rhetoric or modish violence
Deformed a phrase or rhythm; you deferred
To nothing but economy of word.

But that was not the start of it. I had
At seventeen – such a discerning lad! –
Looked for your poems in the library
And found *The Sense of Movement* by Gunn, T.
I read it with mixed feelings, much impressed
By rigour – by the epithets that dressed
Your heroes for attack, more than by what
I now admire as rigour in the thought –
Yet doubting if such toughness was OK
For arty liberals of that latter day.
Then *My Sad Captains* showed me how the wise
Must reason toughly, since they recognise
Unreason in the will, desire and sleep,
And know the limits of the calm they keep.

Soon afterwards we met. I was nineteen
And still a stranger to the poetry scene.
You were in London in the happy year
Of 'Talbot Road', and over pints of beer
Two or three nights we talked of poetry –
Image and metre, gossip and history.
I boasted somewhat, mainly listening though.

Later I realised you'd begun to go
Down new paths to new lines and loyalties:
Looser, though still demanding, more at ease
With what you are and how you have your say.
Famous and thirty-five, your year away
From home and love gave you a second start,
Your learning still unfinished, like your art.

Happy the man of sixty who still sees
Himself as learning! Streetwise Socrates,
You who know nothing and have taught so much,
Twenty-four years now you have kept in touch
Through intermittent letters (meetings rare)
And written off my debts as goods we share.
I tried to imitate your 'mighty line',
Poetic hero, might have made it mine,
Hoping thereby to teach myself a role,
Like you to manufacture my own soul...
Until your new lines, tentative, explored
Like hands in darkness, groping word by word
To touch on things that lie beyond the reach
Of words, though not to wrench them into speech.

Now that our century, blasé with despair,
Broaches its last decade, the troubled air
Trembles with rumour of disastrous ends.
Where you live, with your family of friends,
A plague rules, and it leaves you little choice
But to make death your text, when to rejoice
In ripeness might have suited your old age.
Well, it *is* ripe (since only years assuage
Our grief) to live like you, without regret;
For which I honour you, still in your debt,
And being in part by earlier works consoled:
Those gorgeous metamorphoses, as gold
As California your side of the range,
The sand beyond it undisturbed by change.

1989

Letter to J.A. Cuddon
on his retirement from schoolteaching

Dear Charles,
          I've had you on my mind this year.
A recent shift into the festive gear
Has meant I've seen much more of you, and then
I've found myself reading your books again:
One novel, which you say is not your best
But which has passages – for me the test –
That fixed me to my chair, freezing my arms;
Your *Dictionary of Literary Terms*
(Revised), as good a book for the bedside
As many a novel is; and last, your Guide
To a Jugoslavia scarred with memories
Even in relatively sunlit days.
You raise the question on your opening pages:
How the South Slavs have wrought across the ages
Such violence on each other, and yet face
Strangers with courtesy, tolerance and grace…
Reading I felt at once that the real world
Was there, in those quiet words – and that recalled
School and the way it seemed you never thought
That you were teaching: which is how you taught.
And yes, of course, the other reason why
You've occupied my thoughts is, this July,
You leave the school where – dare I let folks know? –
You taught me more than thirty years ago.

    The model classroom teacher you were not.
If you'd learnt teaching methods, you forgot
To make much use of them: of talk and chalk,
Your preference was plainly for the talk.
Such talk it was! You would, with text in hand,
In gruffly stylish sentences expand
On what we had to read, at times digress,
Not so much analyse. So you'd address –
In Hopkins, say – morphologies of line,
The erotic love that figures the divine,

Grey falcons stooping, the Ignatian rule,
Forms literary and biological –
All of the things, in short, I wished to know
Or thought I should, once you had sketched them so.

    You did your job, then, also coached a team
(Rugby or cricket), but did not ever seem
Quite *of* the school. Our *Führer* of a Head
(You wryly told me) used to cut you dead
In the corridor – or else you'd be required
At once to see your barber. I *admired*
What must have niggled him: your tattered gown,
The perpetual cigarette, and the slight frown
(Not without humour) that told less of care
Than of the mental life you lived elsewhere –
The books and journeys out beyond the gate
At the drive's end. Indeed, you turned up late
Each autumn term – though just in time to teach –
Tanned like a bather on a southern beach,
Having come (went the rumour) straight to school
From the last sleeper out of Istanbul.

    I would not say that you were dissident –
Just that, maybe, a habit of dissent
Showed in your conduct. For you spared the rod
And if, to our surprise, you talked of God,
Yours was a Roman cosmopolitan,
Who made the Chaplain's by comparison
Seem a provincial… Be that as it may,
For me these sparks ignited in a play:
How well do you remember *The Dumb Waiter?*
Some consternation in the *alma mater*
Was caused by your production of it: *hard*
It seemed in '62, too *avant-garde*
And Beckettishly weird. What did it *mean?*
Was there perhaps a god in that machine?
Did he exact day-labour, light denied?
Were blasphemies like Pinter's justified
By *deeper meanings?* Such fatuity

Seemed to your actors – just Steve Gooch and me –
Appalling, though no doubt outraged surprise
Fed our young vanities. You, worldly wise,
Grunted ironically – you would, of course –
And on the last night led us, after hours,
Up to the staff room where your *bonhomie*
Invited us to share a fine Chablis.
This disinclined us to take much to heart
Those slight distresses which the life of art
Inflicts on its adherents: it's a test
That poet, novelist and dramatist
Must pass before they ripen. Don't complain
Of losses, wordsmith; drink deep when you gain.

   A wordsmith, Charles. That strikes me as a fair
Description of you, yet I'm well aware
That earlier I spoke of gruffness too.
I mean a reticence I find in you –
Not unbecoming in a soldier's son –
Which edges all your words. I think of one
Lesson when you contrasted styles of verse.
The note of conversation, plain and terse,
Was what you favoured. The luxuriant –
In music as in sensuous ornament –
You admired too, for richness and for skill,
But had your reservations. I can still
Hear you chastise as *facile* and as *glib*
The sort of bard who runs off at the nib.
New to me at that age, the two words stuck
As you had used them, emblems of my luck
In being taught by one whose words were weighed
Like ingots of great price; and this has made
You present in those words whenever, since,
I've found them used precisely in that sense.
That, I suppose, is what it is to teach –
Not only how to use words but that speech
Is difficult. We use words to mean things,
And something more than that which soothes and sings
Informs good poems – they are answerable

To fact, which is resistant to the will.
I learnt from you to value stubbornness
And to judge best those works that bear the impress
Of silence in their margins. Can't you see
How I must fight to ward off fluency? –
For instance in this letter here, which I've
Composed in celebration. Believe me,

                                        Clive

                                                    1993

In Memoriam Graham Davies, Psychotherapist (1937–1993)

You, invisible, once again, I address.
I almost seem to welcome the distress
That puts me back in touch with you once more.
Remember how I called you 'my old whore'
And how you laughed at that? – for, young or old,
Whores charge for love, even those with hearts of gold.
So you charged and I loved. And though you'd try
To justify the fact, I had to lie
On the same couch where other clients had lain.
Our play was serious, yet it was quite plain
That all the passion in it came from me.
You tricked me out of feeling solitary
By being others for me. That way, you
Were priest as well as healer, teacher too,
And father. My dead father. *You* are dead
They tell me, Graham. This is now my head
We talk in and I cannot turn to reach
The man behind the couch whose flights of speech
Lodged in my own, much as his garden birds
Merged with its foliage. Even now your words
Stay with me: I can hear your sympathy
And irritation, your lucidity
And warmth, your massive knowledge, your quiet laugh…

You had, framed in your hall, a photograph
I loved – it was of the Christ Pantocrator
From Vézelay, sculpted there above the door.
He gazed impassively into the minds
Of all who entered. Lapped by rushing winds,
Harried by turbulence, huge hands aflame,
He sits in judgement there. He is the same
In wrath or love, stern judge or gentle son.
His is the tranquil character of stone,
Hard and unmoving, sensuous, warmed by light,
Changeless, yet, suffering the chisel's bite,
Yielding to what it images: the soul.

That was your business. In a different role –
Traveller, pilgrim, call it what you will –
You stare from a snap-shot. You don't look ill
Exactly, but somehow edgy, as you half
Turn from the hands that clinched the photograph
Toward the horizon – anxious to be gone…
At least, so it would seem to anyone
Who knew this was the day before you died.
The camera might have caught you in mid-stride
There by the cliff's edge, making for the sea,
Which, struck by light, almost transcendently
Blurs into sky in one pale silver blaze.
They found you in mid-stride, but with your gaze
Turned inward and your body on the ground
Still plunging out across Iona Sound
Toward the heave of mountain, it would seem,
Vision outpacing sense, Elijah's team
Already harnessed to the chariot-shaft
And pawing the clouds.
                              Where you were photographed
In fact was Staffa, but you went to die,
The next day, on Iona, where the sky
And land seem more akin, I'm told; for there
Beach, field and outcrop are a single layer
Laid thinly on the water, and the land's
Transparent frailty timelessly withstands

The ocean's grim authority. I know
Places like that. In them the spirit so
Permeates all the common world with thought
They bear the traces of a different sort
Of journey to one's own. Unreconciled
To your departures, I was like a child
Who won't believe his elders quite exist
Outside his orbit. You went south and east
As well as north, but always you returned –
As elders do. When, like a boy who's learned,
I felt the strength to travel on my own,
You stabilised in my thought, settling like stone.
We'd meet at concerts. Do you recall that voice –
A pure soprano, firm yet tenuous –
We heard, in a bare chapel, make lament
Without vibrato or accompaniment
For a crusader love? We followed where
It gave at last on silence and thin air,
Ending as if intended to go on,
Lost in the space it filled.
                                        Where have you gone?
Where have you *all* gone, who are invisible?
Into the world of light? Or have you all
Turned inwards, melting into thought instead?
Or vanished? Graham, when I saw you dead,
And saw my mother dead, you were both mere
Things, as desks and chairs are things, no more
Life in you than in stolid wood that once
Stirred all through with the rich circumstance
Of wind and weather. Yet the leaves still sprout
In the mind's branchings, tenderly reaching out
For light as the birds come, nestle there and stay.
I point to them. You comment. What you say
Is much like what you said, though in this way,
Somehow, you teach me more. I always knew
The richness of the mind, saw how it grew
Through all the human seasons, how it fed
On all the variousness outside the head;
And yet I never could accommodate

Its quirks, its weirder vagaries, the dull hate
Its warmest love includes, its sullen sluice
Of loathsome wants, the intermingled juice
Of painfullest secretions, how its strange
Flirtations with the arbitrary derange
And dissipate. Recoiling from that mess,
I looked instead for grace and shapeliness
And luminosity. So how much stranger
It now seems that, today, I feel less danger
From that – having looked into it with you –
Than I could have imagined. Stranger, too,
That the great world seems grander and the mind
Richer, more luminous – thought more refined
By being sieved through talk, more prone to form
For all those crazed departures from the norm.

But in the darkness, when I face your loss
And see my journey as it always was,
Unfinished, thwarted and circuitous,
I doubt the powers I trusted, I resent
The pain, hard cash and energy I spent
On the long quest, I feel the tender scars
Reopen now, and the old tide of fears
Comes in around me... Then, to my surprise,
I find that I am back with you, my eyes
A-birding through your window, and your voice
Lighting on this occasion to rejoice
In requiem – I feel it on my scalp,
A *cantus firmus* which I cannot help
But build on polyphonically, the world
Eluding us as we, with word on word,
Elaborate upon infinity –
Such magnitude, such multiplicity,
So simple. Graham, I first came to you
Unable to believe it quite untrue
That great creating nature was divine.
I am none the wiser. But, now you resign
Your part in that great argument and turn
Half-way away from me, I seem to learn

That, being dead, you *are* what I now know.
So I consult you, hoping that way to grow
A better man, and so you speak to me,
Not from the throne of Vézelay, vertically,
But from the shadows that I leave behind me.
Like them, it is of myself that you remind me –
Though you remain the trusted friend no less,
Whom, though invisible, I again address.

1993

III

Visitation

Who are you that have stepped into the light
            so unforeseeably
            that 'goddess' seems the word?
                        how else to name

that beauty more than beauty, inwardness
            so perfectly made flesh
            we are abased by it
                        and almost fear

there will be no way back – though to come back,
            the vision thus relinquished,
            is what we least desire?
                        I most desire

you here and now, although, till here and now,
            I could not yet have wanted
            what still remained unknown –
                        except, we're told,

there'd be no dream of earthly paradise
            without the fallen earth.
            Your body is a thing
                        as the earth is

but with the fragrance of another world…
            O gentle girl, who tremble
            when you are touched, whom I
                        tremble to touch,

you rend the dark like lightning, leaving day
            solemn with ravage, yet
            bright with the evidence
                        of visitation.

The Heron

The heron nests in the mountains:
she takes to the heights, no bird
can reach as high as she can,
she is not to be touched.

My anxious thought has found
her refuge out, but still
the more you make pursuit,
the more she fends you off.
For me it is enough
to follow her and hold her
in view, for the eye's pleasure.
She is not to be held.

Many have followed her
thinking to take her, yet
whoever finds himself
closest is first forgotten.
What more could a man desire
than but to look on her,
devotion thus repaid?
She is not to be grasped.

I have never seen a creature
so fine, so elegant,
so far beyond possessing.
From her great height she disdains
all men who hope; and therefore,
being so beautiful,
she makes the world her captive.
She, though, will not be caught.

after Juan del Encina

Vacations

for M.L.

Look: snow on Helvellyn's peak
at Christmas time. How the cold shines!
  How, stooped by their white burden,
    bare trees sway over hard lakes!

Nothing for it but to heap the blaze
with more logs and, in genial mood,
  bring out your darkest wine,
    its summer heat four winters old.

What brought us here, frost in our hair?
What wrecked your ship? Broke down my roof?
  Let be: before too long,
    seas will be tranquil, trees tall.

As for tomorrow – what it will bring –
put that and regret aside. For now,
  think each new day pure gain –
    just as it is for those whose bloom

is freshly upon them, who can't envision
their own sweetness. Watch them at dusk
  spill out into warm streets
    where jasmine twines with honeysuckle,

then hear, as from a gurgling spring,
the laughing murmurs of a girl
  beyond the streetlamp's arc:
    how she croons *No, no,* without resisting.

after Horace

To Pyrrha

What skinny lad, sweet-smelling, rubbed with oil,
has got you where he wants you, couched with roses
        down there in your snug nook?
   Is it for him you braid your blond hair

in careless elegance? Poor boy, how often
will he protest at change in fate and women,
        shocked at a sea turned rough
   as the dark winds bear down on it,

though he enjoys you now – thinking you gold
all through, lovely forever, your desires
        forever fixed on him –
   and hears no breeze stirring. For all

who are struck by you untried, it's a grim outlook.
And me? I long ago took out a policy
        that charges a heavy premium
   on shipwrecks and other acts of God.

after Horace

Soft and Hard Porn

1. *Artemis*

You turn the page

she steps out
of the bath, she looks
from her long reflection
back at you

humbling you,
those eyes
as of a god

Light answers
from her lips'
red gloss
and from points of
the tumbling
hair her left arm's
raised to hold up

So that you note
the trenched sweep of
the spine, so elegant,
the fruit-round rump and
from under the armpit the
weight and sway
of a breast, the nipple unseen

except in the mirror
beneath
that baleful stare

2. *Persephone*

        dark interior
the opening pierced with gems

        bright
against that setting of
        spread lips

it begins here the feeling journey

        hers
a nomad privacy
        framed
all her wealth displayed

Fin de Siècle
Montmartre, 1890s

Don't look, but the sun is setting, and the leaves
Out there on the silver birches have turned gold:
You can almost *hear* them, jangling in the wind!
Why not paint that? Oh but you see, I do –
Searching your curves and hollows, yet with this
Decay staining the atmosphere, this chill,
This fog in the soul's crevices.

And then, you know, I regard you with desire,
Which is the desire of art, and that includes
The desire for it to end, for you to leave
And for the night to come.
                                            Well, shall I go
To *The Green Monkey* for the *décolletage*
Of that girl who hangs around there, the gas-light
Finding a coarser gold between her breasts
As it burns lips and cheeks a fiercer red?
Or to the gilded dark of *Sacré Coeur*
Where I can light a candle and attend
To the drone of Vespers, conscious that outside
The last rays yield crushed russet to grey ash?

But that's already to have gone too far.
I like this moment, now:
This is the time when, work my compelling passion,
I nonetheless start longing. For what else?
Not to stop work but for something to be there
When the work stops. Moments, by definition,
End – without ending there can be no meaning,
No picture without frame.

So here, your chemise, your stockings, and all that –
Just let me wash this brush. Thank you, I share
Your pleasure in it. Though I have you here,
It's always inward too, an act of mind –
Just knowing how you look

Where you're not seen, watching the light pass
And labouring to catch one moment of it
To make your moment, charged with other times.

As for me, what I've been working for
Comes when you've left, although it couldn't come
If you had not been here. My muffler on,
I'll saunter down to watch the afterglow
Beyond the cemetery, as way beneath
Paris puts on her evening dress, her jewels
Flickering more acutely for the dark.

The New Era
A lake near Dresden, 1910

In *The New Era* coffee house, that's where.
Reinhard was with you, and he came across
To interrupt my reading. You can't, I think,
Have noticed me: by then you were too deep
In conversation with – what *is* her name? –
Your flirty friend. But me, once I had seen you,
I couldn't keep my eyes off. I can't now.
Which is as well in one who's painting you –
More lovely here in the pure light of day
Than in the gas-lamp's aura; though for me
As I paint now, the sun being so intense,
You struggle with the shadows and I fight
To guard you from those stark contrastive schemes
That coarsen. As I say, later that night,
Dear Reinhard took you home and, in a sort
Of trance, I followed, keeping to the dark.
I mooned around outside your house until
The lights went out. It was then that everything
Inside me, like a forest of dry shrubs,
Caught fire and the flames leapt from branch to branch
Till I was white with heat.

To cool the blaze
I set out walking, dawn my only goal,
And with no thought of them I came upon
The ladies of the night, there on the *Platz*,
Hugging the streetlamps in their fissured clouds
Of smoke and frosted breath.
No, dearest, no,
It wasn't that but, rather, up till then
What had I painted but those mournful girls,
Hair down in dark cascades, and brooding knights,
Their chainmail meshed with thorny briars, each rose
Impeccably itself? These were real.
They were everything I had not yet touched.
They strutted like exotic birds – bright plumage
And faces brighter than my palette is
That spoke to me of my work.
Therefore it seems
They and not Reinhard brought me to these dunes
Here by the lake where this your nakedness
Is pure and paradisal, so that Adam
Can roam again among the clumps of growth,
Now free to sample. Yes, we will have change.
I'll give what we can see these wilder hues –
Gold flesh on purple waves with crimson sky –
And draw a blueprint for the time to come.
We are making a new world.

IV

Epitaph
M.A.B.B. (1925–1996)

Why do the robin and the butterfly
Linger where you have lingered? Can they know
The knowledge, wit and charity that lie
Here now and yet go with you where you go?

At a Friend's Funeral
In Memoriam: Michael Bulkley

Parce, Domine, enim nihil sunt dies mei

Spare me, Lord, for my days are nothing.

My friend, though, who is not here as I am,
Is everywhere and in all things.

What is it binds us then?
                              Nothing but words –
This reading, this incantation, this great cry,
These voices woven in polyphony
Unwoven into silence.

Tomorrow, only the words in my head
As my days unpick themselves, till they are nothing.

Fernando Pessoa's Lisbon

1. *Flat*

Plain, square, modern, small:
room enough, it would seem,
for the populous brain.

2. *Bar*

Black ink, green liquor:
how the mind
poisons the indivisible flesh.

Wood Work
In Memoriam: Henri Gaudier-Brzeska (1891–1915)

1

Henri Gaudier

from an enemy
rifle-butt
carved

Caritas
an infant
at each dug

condemned to die

2

gouge
      into wood grain
against
      gun metal

in tempore belli
      Pax

Stone Work
Floor tomb, Santa Croce, Florence

Cut in stone
        coat and hood
fall from him
        in the folds of sleep.

The good mind
        has made its mark
in the pillow,
        a slight impress.

More gradual
        than forgetting is,
steps passing
        efface features.

A Baroque Concerto
to Edgar Bowers, at 70

'Pure mathematics!' That's what you exclaimed
Across the polite applause to me, enthused
By a forgotten opus hardly famed
In its own time or place. Not being used
To seeing you moved and vulnerable then brought
Another harmony into my head,
The divisions of your verse, its metres taut,
Drawn from the order trusted to the dead.

A love of the abstract … yet you evoke,
Through poignant scenes of Europe sketched in youth,
An order that's the sharper for the smoke;

And, later on, make your locality –
The golden coastline where civility
Encounters nature – witness to the truth.

1994

Casa Natal de Borges

...a man who, in an age that worships the chaotic idols of blood, earth and passion, preferred... the lucid pleasures of thought and the secret adventures of order.

Borges on Valéry

The secret adventures of order
Began in this emblem of the *Belle Epoque*:
The orderly elegance of the *haut-bourgeois*,
Who have secrets but few adventures.

Lost to its old seclusion, smeared with grime,
It endures quotidian rage, an inhuman alarm
And in shop windows intimacies laid bare.
It persists, though,
Like the last, yellowing, undecayed incisor
In a mouth whose gleaming beauty is long gone.

The city as *locus* of civility:
An accident of time perhaps? But time
Moves on and leaves behind it
An invisible city, continuing, made of messages
Strung together by those who have most cherished
The lucid pleasures of thought.

Buenos Aires, 1999

The Translator's Apology
for Patrick McGuinness

I have been faithful to the text, after my own fashion.
There have been other adventures, other assignations,
Over and over, with words mouthed and whispered.
But I am faithful in spirit.
If I have gone astray,
If I have deviated into paraphrase,
If I have gone half mad with imitation,
It has always been that some other dusky beauty
Reflected the original, a transitory embodiment.
Forgive me! Truth is my real goal.
Who that laid hands on that perfect form
Could do other than stay with that in perfect constancy?

Olivier Messiaen

1. *Wilderness*

What is it this cacophony,
this concord of sounds, some sweet,
some not so sweet? It is
the order of things.

The wingbeat of Bonelli's eagle,
a thunderclap, the song of the hermit thrush,
the city at night – zigzag of siren and horn,
the whoosh of the desert wind.

Terrible is this place: it is
the house of God, the gate of heaven.

2. *Cathedral*

To read by analogy: columns,
Like tree-trunks, disclose light;
Birds, in the foliate capitals,
Are wide-billed amid fruit

But silent, until *this*
Radiates through it all.
Then the birds sing, the leaves hiss,
Wind shushes, though air is still.

3. *Revelation*

you who, in what is made of time, end time...

     hatched out of dissonance,
the single, held, unending chord or chime...

THE MYSTERY OF THINGS

(2006)

TO THE MEMORY OF MASTERS AND FRIENDS

Donald Davie
Charles Cuddon
Michael Bulkley
Tony Tanner
Edgar Bowers
Thom Gunn

ché 'n la mente m'è fitta, e or me accora,
la cara e buona imagine paterna
di voi quando nel mondo ad ora ad ora

m'insegnavate come l'uom s'etterna;
e quant'io l'abbia in grado mentr'io vivo
convien che nella mia lingua si scerna.

INFERNO XV

…for in my memory is fixed – now it pierces my heart – the dear, kind, paternal image I have of you, when in the world, hour by hour, you taught me how man makes himself eternal; and it is right and proper that, as long as I live, my gratitude for that is shown in my language.

I

[We'll] take upon's the mystery of things
As if we were God's spies

KING LEAR

Bottom's Dream

It shall be called 'Bottom's Dream', because it hath no bottom…

I was a weaver, and I wove
The moody fabric of my dream.
By day I laboured at the loom
And glimpsed the image of a love
       I now know bottomless.

We were young men. We played our parts.
We schooled ourselves in the quiet wood.
By night the moon, which draws the flood,
Tugged at the rhythms of our hearts.
       And they were bottomless.

I loved a girl who was a boy;
I took my stand and beat my breast.
Yet what was I but fool and beast,
Who did not so much speak as bray,
       In bombast bottomless?

I trusted I had mastery,
Until one night, being left alone,
I snorted at the wandering moon
In terror of the mystery,
       Which seemed quite bottomless,

And out of that *she* spoke, who had
No voice, although she stirred my sense,
Who touched me, though she had no hands,
And led me where you cannot lead,
       Since it is bottomless.

I tried to speak: again I brayed.
I pinched and scratched my face: coarse hairs
Were crisping over cheeks and ears.
And when she drew me in, she made
       The whole world bottomless.

Nothing possessed me. So she said
Do not desire to leave this wood.
Among the mossy clefts I hid
With petals where she pressed my head,
       Desire being bottomless.

A most rare vision, such a thing
As who should say what such things be:
My terror turned to ecstasy,
The one much like the other, being
       Both of them bottomless.

And then the change. The sun came up
Brash as a brassy hunting-horn.
I woke and, yes, I was a man.
Was I myself though? Self, like sleep,
       May well be bottomless.

New moon tonight. Another dream
To act. They laugh at our dismay.
Oh but it's nothing. Only play.
Except we just don't feel the same,
       For play is bottomless.

And so the story ends. My eyes
Are sore with weeping, but I laugh
(I who was seen to take my life),
For, having been an ass, I'm wise
       And bottomless. Bottomless.

Dog Rose in June

Pink petals flare in the hedge:
Rosa canina, rose of the dog days.
Gently I splay the petals, bend and sniff.
The whole flower gives off sweetness,
Pungency deeper in.
Such heat this evening, come away from the path.

Wonderwoman

I lay where I had fallen
Naked on the floor, alone, unable to stand –
And waited for the ambulance. This was to mean
Complete surrender to another's will.

She appeared at the window-sill
And dropped in over the top half of the sash:
Pale blond hair drawn back, sand-white at the brow,
And eyes like summer sky
And a gold tan running deep into her cleavage
And a perfume something to do with flowers and the salt smell of
                                                              the sea.

I felt the discourtesy
Of not rising to greet her. Nonetheless,
She gathered me up, bore me almost, carried me away.
What could I do?
I was like Odysseus in Circe's arms, enthralled,
But in my helplessness
Not quite believing I was not a pig,
And yet knowing myself, inside myself,
Moved to my best of inwardness.

Greensleeves

O my love is like an
Out-of-tune ice-cream van.

In the Library

You at your book. Me unable to read,
supposing that I get between your words
as, fingers twined in your hair or stroking your neck,
    you nonetheless read on.

Since you will not answer letters or calls
or nod to me in the street, I will write to the moon
or else to the image I have of you in my mind,
    which is all responsiveness.

Either way, fearing that I might touch,
you fend me off by scowling into a book;
but I'm there among the words, wanting to be,
    like them, read into you.

The Ruin

Cattle browse in the meadow the sprung arch,
shot of its tracery, frames

Form looking out of ruin, a different view
shaped by the form's persistence
                      Miracle,
no other word for it, the enduring face
of Andrei Rublyov's *Saviour*, gazing out
from what, after several centuries as a doorstep,
the context gone, is plainly still a board:
not Christ the judge, this one – a hurt survivor
with knowledge it is hard to look away from
of what is suffered here
                And come again
as Radnóti's last poems from the dark
and warmth of a mass grave, which they had shared
with swathes of greatcoat and corrupting flesh,

till brought to light
                              So the old bagwoman,
raddled, incontinent, hoists her reeking skirts
and, her lips pursed for crooning, rasps aloud:
Paradise, boys, come on, you can have it now.

Much Ado about Nothing

signifying
                    a lot of fuss about fucking
or even about that primal quantity
known in those days as *naught*, as naughty,
as NO THING:
                    calling to mind
Courbet's *L'Origine de l'univers.*

For nothing this wide universe I call
– know what I mean? –
in it thou art my all

and all for nothing.
For nothing doing. Since nothing
shall come of nothing.
                              Yea,
do on then this nought
else that thou do it for God's love and
nothing have these nothings if this be nothing
that is not there;
                    and the Nothing that is
our inner man clepeth All.

The Holy of Holies

            then broke in and found nothing.

She took me by the hand. A desolate place,
a place of stones, being unmade and made:
dark gashes in the earth with, all about,
stagnant pools, so churned up the terrain;
and standing alone, a stark new office-block,
half-built and bare, its concrete white in the moon.

From destruction we may draw consolation:
that there's no escape from fate,
not for great works or even holy places.
Nevertheless, that so ravishing a building,
its materials alone – marble and cedarwood –
so sumptuous, the stone so smoothly cut
so closely joined

            Think of that
and, thinking of the place, how deep inside, there
in the Holy of Holies,
you can lose what you are,
desire to, fear to

           As I Flavius,
a soldier of fortune, not myself a Roman,
in this epoch since the fall,
trafficked with a lithe avatar of the goddess
Astarte, Aphrodite, whatever name,
in the region of King's Cross.
She it was
who led me through that place to the tall block
as yet unfinished, so that it seemed a ruin

the sanctum, the broken chancel, the lopped shaft
holier than it would have been
intact

before it, bare and empty, a white lodge,
a simple cube of space, and we went in.
One window, the moon seen through it, and the night
unseasonably warm, she threw her dress aside,
breasts and shoulders silvered by the moonlight:
she was so beautiful I could have
gone down on my knees but, as we stood there,
I ran my fingertips along her mouth, caressed
her nipples, the dome of her belly, the dark fuzz:
I thought and measured, seeking
the precise gentleness to weigh the value.

These two together.

                  Flavius
saw the Temple burn in Jerusalem,
saw it fall, with ravines for its foundations,
the superstructure not unworthy of them,
their depth, their great magnificence, their strength.
Nevertheless it fell,
the Temple of Solomon and the house of wisdom
waxed marble and scented cedarwood
fell
at the touch of flame.

The torches carved a space out of the darkness,
a recess of twenty cubits, until then
screened by a veil and unapproachable,
inviolable, invisible to all.
In it stood nothing whatever, it was called
the Holy of Holies

        lose what you are
            fear   desire

dark
        made darker still by the white ray:
she turned away from me, as if to bow
to the moon's face, but leaned on the rough sill,

so that her breasts hung softly in my hands

then the flames flared and leapt,
I pushed lightly and the entrance gave

Recorded Message

Here for your pleasure –
no rush –
day by day:

Dawn
Summer
Celeste

Amber
Dolores
Caprice

and Crystal
or, sometimes,
Precious.

A Vision

'In a doorway, I swear.
                    There were these two –
I was late cycling home
                    a gorgeous night
midsummer and people
                    out partying still.
I freewheeled past this shop
                    they were necking there
but she had her breasts out

one hand on his fly.
The bike sailed breezily on –
                    I did a sort of
drawn-out double-take,
                    turned back up the hill
and there she was
                    on her knees now
blowing his horn.
                    Imagine
how I felt:
                    like some Sicilian peasant
hailed one day
                    by an angel on the dung-heap –
or this girl walking ahead
                    in a blue scarf
turns to accost him, he stares
                    and it's the Virgin.
They're funny, Catholics: so
                    literal sometimes
about the things of the spirit,
                    even fleshly.'

The Ladder

… this any *place where God lets down the ladder*
                                        John Ruskin

'Don't let go yet. What was it made you cry
Just then? Keep holding on to me. You cried
Like a new baby launched upon the world,
A singer at her pitch of ecstasy,
A trapped animal howling against pain.'

I cried?
            'As if from a shut room inside.
Not like your own: like someone else's cry

Sounding within you.'
                              If it was me that cried,
Or if through me the two of us, it was
That as we grappled here we seemed to touch
Some nerve of inwardness. Let me turn preacher.
I have, in former discourse, been inclined
To speak of love as though it were a thing
Outward and visible: the which thing is
In truth a fallacy. Consider Jacob,
Who wrestled with an angel and prevailed.
Where was that angel? Or those other ones
He witnessed in a nameless desert place
Somewhere between Beersheba and Haran?
The scriptures use the figure of a ladder
Propped between land and sky to body forth
The dream he had, head pillowed on a stone,
Of angel hosts ascending and descending.
But now, from the new exegetes, we learn
Of a stark outcrop glacially planed,
A table-land, with terracing for stairs;
Or – since it was, he said, the House of God –
Of a stepped temple, a symbolic mount
Like a vast altar, from whose surface priests,
With cries to distant gods, offered up smoke,
Throwing it forth, as charred bones fell away,
A frail and ghostly bridge from earth to heaven.

'We have travelled a long way
From the dark chamber of your inwardness.
What could have caused that resonance today?'

I don't know. It was nothing. I can't say.

Bethel

When Jacob in the desert stopped
   For nightfall and the climbing stars,
He slept, a stone his pillow,
     Among volcanic scars.

He saw the angels of the Lord
   Ascending and descending there
In glory, with the Lord himself
     Above the topmost stair.

At break of day he set the stone
   An upright pillar on the ground.
It made the sky a heavenly roof
     And earth's foundation sound.

The Architect at his Mountain Villa

All I can do is take you to the edge
     And throw a belvedere
Out on the void, fenced in with cabled steel,
So there is nothing which you need to fear –
     As fear you will,
Like somebody marooned on a rock ledge.

This is what builders do: compose a space
     For you to live inside
And be in body. They can give no more
Than wood or concrete, stone or brick provide.
     All else they ignore,
Except to make a view out of a place.

What if the view were merely space? What if
        Odd atmospheric freaks –
Stray clouds, perhaps a viscous film of mist –
Were all that filled it? Floating, the snow peaks
        Barely exist –
Far less than we do, grounded in this cliff.

For my Daughter's Wedding
to Tamsin and Chris, with love

A photograph. It is a woodland place
In late spring and a girl of two or three
Looks at the camera with an earnest face
That might have just been smiling. Could that be
Fear in those soft eyes? No, it is rather trust,
Though trust derives from some first sense of fear.
But still, the woods are tranquil and buds thrust
Expansively into the genial air.

The child is now a woman who today
Turns the same earnest look toward her love,
Then laughs, her head thrown back, in her dear way.
Such fun. Such seriousness. You know them, Chris:
They make rough places kindly and they save
Our world from what might be sheer wilderness.

14 July 2000

Overnight Snow

There are star-crystals shining white on the blank earth.
It is a visitation from on high,
Where there is nothing but exploding worlds
And radiant fragments of infinity.

Plenty

Apples,
     as if they were blossoms,
         left to drop.

Chutney
for Lyubomir Nikolov

Apples: they clogged the brook,
and the turf under the boughs
was a cobbled yard to our feet:
     do you remember?

How returning at dusk we rescued
four plastic-bagsful of them –
so ripe they were, and bruised,
     and near to rotting.

We cooked them in vinegar
with onions, garlic, sultanas,
soft brown sugar, ground ginger,
     salt and black pepper.

Jar after jar for gifts.
Yet I'm eating it still, and still
I've a store, which stores in itself
     that fruitful September –

you remember it, Lyubomir,
     I know you remember.

The Apple Trees
for Lyubomir Nikolov, again

But the trees, Lyubomir, remember the trees!
Five or six of them, each a distinct variety
Of apple – yellow or red, russet or buff-green –
With a footbridge over the brook
And a path winding among them through high grass.

One I can still see.
In the mind's eye, as then through the body's too,
I feel the gravid pull
Of the fruit bunched red among green, red as the autumn sun,
Bending the boughs.

Well, now they are gone.
Churning up rights of way,
Bulldozers plough the earth for the new block.
New rights, of course, will succeed the old, but for what?
There is always something more important than trees.

What is anger, my friend, but a form of memory?
I will not let go.
To do so, I know (so they tell me), is good for the soul.
I cannot think of that. I prefer the pain of knowing the trees lost
To losing the trees.

At Great Coxwell

Great Coxwell tithe barn (William Morris said)
'As noble as a great cathedral' – and
On the same mighty scale.
                                        Arriving there
One incandescent afternoon, we saw
In the arrow-slit just over the main portal
A carrion crow alighting. It then flew

A dipping flight the length of the dark hall
To pass, without a feint at hesitation,
Out through the other slit at the far end,
The white glare momentarily gone black:

Like Bede's sparrow, with a grimmer touch.

Behold, the Fowls of the Air
for Ingrid Soren, Buddhist & Christian

1

The world is sunk in darkness.
The great light is seen by few of us.
Few birds escape the net;
Few souls attain the freedom beyond night.

2

The city judged, the red kite and the bittern
Lay claim to it, the screech-owl and the raven
Haunt the streets, the tumbled stones of chaos
Mark out the borders of its emptiness.

3

The stork on the chimney-stack knows when to leave;
Likewise, the crane, the swallow and the dove
Watch for their time. We, though, shade our eyes;
When judgement falls, it falls to our surprise.

4

Those who, young, were inwardly at war
Missed the real treasure that eludes desire.
In age, they are like the heron – lank, unfed –
By a pool empty of fish. They look sad.

5

Consider the birds of the air:
They neither reap nor sow nor store,
And yet your Father feeds them day by day.
You are, surely, more than they.

6

Even the sparrow has found a home,
And the nesting swallow room
Just near the altar of my God and King,
Where she may raise her young.

7

Is it by your wisdom and at your word
That the hawk flies, that she spreads her wings southward?
Did you bid the eagle tower? And can you brag
She builds her rough nest on the topmost crag?

8

Flight is the miracle that frees the swan
To follow the sun's path. Strong men
First conquer evil and its troops, then soar
Above the narrow space where they made war.

9

Two sparrows make a pennyworth,
Yet if just one of them should fall to earth,
Your Father knows. Your every hair
He has numbered. Do not fear.

10

The swift forsakes her home. She sweeps south,
In her wake the dark and cold, like bitter truth.
Yet she returns. Soon you will hear her wail,
As if in agony, that all is well.

Sources: *Dhammapada* 13.174; Isaiah 34.11; Job 39.26–28; *Dhammapada* 11.155;
Matthew 6.26; Psalms 84.3; Jeremiah 8.7; *Dhammapada* 13.175; Matthew 10.29–31

In the Beginning

In
PRINCIPIO
the Evangelist
rapt in contemplation of the Word,
an eagle at his ear, his slender wrist
poised over the page, the bird poised,
contemplative, predatory, for the long flight.

This is the record of John, as of the scribe
in the monks' scriptorium on the green isle
some fourteen hundred years ago, at the edge
of the known world – that world, margin to centre,
the unerring flight of a migratory bird.

Then, facing the illumination, blocks
of language, columns, they might be towers of stone
to withstand siege and temporal incursion,
born of the air, though, to be borne on air,
as on broad wings, migrating into time.

And this, the record of stone, a fine-grained
Bavarian limestone, it splits into thin slabs,
creamy and smooth – pages that, once turned,
disclose the print of fortune, left unread
a hundred-and-fifty million years and more.

It is Archaeopteryx, in the beginning,
cresting the wave of time, those first feathers
lifting it, buoying it on, until catastrophe
set it down, the molten instant set,
process, not progress, still less final form.

The gaping mouth, teeth bared, the pinions splayed,
nailed to that moment there, eternity
its inconceivable frame: this hieroglyph –
whose language, never held in mind, is silent –
launched upon prophecy, utters itself.

W.S. Graham Reading

Word drunk they called him. Well:
I don't know about *words*.
                    He sat there turning the pages
unable to fix on a single verse
plaintive and truculent
                    quarrelling with the book,
as if to surrender to a single instance
of language
                    was to surrender.

Then: 'Read any one of them,' somebody cried:
'They're all marvellous!'
                    And we beheld a marvel:
an Archangel
                    a little damaged
igniting the dark firmament with speech.

To George Herbert

Time and again I turn to you, to poems
In which you turn from vanity to God
Time and again, as I at the line's turn
Turn through the blank space that modulates –
And so resolves – the something that you say.

The Source

Not far from here, though hidden, is the source.
Imagine the threads of water as they run
Over the silty bank they issue from
To join the current they will reinforce.

What need for origin? The river might
Bite its own tail in one unending 'o'
Without beginning, and we need not know
Where it first came from, nor where it will go.

The source is nothing, yet the source is there,
And but to think is to return to where
Nothing became something, as meaning words
In utterance. You can pursue your course
Without reflection, and yet once to ask
'What is the river?' is to think the source.

The Falls
for Jim Spates

I am haunted by this memory of the falls:
The turbulent water with its bloom of froth
      Hung like a curtain, still
      Changeless and invariable;
Yet spat and spumed, dripped and cascaded, gushed –
Eased itself of the burden the great lakes
      Had urged upon it. Also,
      Viewed from the side, it stood
From the rock wall like a sheer and polished pane
At the top curved and stooping to the plunge –
      To the deep catastrophe
      That shattered it – and then
Rebounded back as star-flung spray, a deathless
Tower of it, rising, as if in worship –

              *

Did Jackson Pollock
                    when he painted *One*
know the Lord's beauty by it?
                              What we call
randomness –
              the white stream
lashed over brown and purple
                            sprayed and flecked –
not at all
          deep canyons of the underself
but the order in which things fall
                  or what intelligence will make of them.
Draped from the rock it
                        frills but falls:
the same pattern, never
                        the same water.
You will find
             (I must tell you)
no great man
            not a man of law.

                              *

Further downstream we had paused at other falls:
Slight trickles, graceful cataracts, rapids, weirs,
          The still rock around which
          A rope of current tugged
And, frothing from some ledge, a watery fringe
Of tasselled elegance. Each one of them,
          For all the vehement clamour,
          Displayed rule and design;
Though they fell, they fell by the same laws,
And all such law breeds pattern. This one, however,
          Was quite another thing:
          A gulf in the earth's crust,
Chaos to us – ocean or milky way –
And order, therefore, in the larger mind.

                              *

the sun and the other stars
the beating heart
the snow-melt

driven, crying
of this steep place afraid
the common pass

but fraying there
the vast drum of woven stuff unwinding,
the dripped lace

no measure fine enough
eye or finger or numerate brain

immutable change
made and remade
laws finer than any known of men

from things made
being seen and understood
the invisible things

each frill and fibre
eternal power

II

TO ROSAMOND

For nothing this wide universe I call
Save thou, my rose; in it thou art my all.

SHAKESPEARE, SONNET 109

Ghostliness

1

The host
steeped in wine
limp on my tongue,

I, for the
first time,
tasted flesh,

all day thereafter
haunted
by the ghost.

2

You beside me
sharing
the ghostly taste,

your flesh
has come so close
there is no flesh

and no spirit,
only
the twining ghosts.

Stigmata

as thou art
All my delight, so all my smart

George Herbert

I
The Visit to La Verna

Holiness, not wholeness. If I touched
Too fiercely, just a shade so, you would bleed,
So near the skin your innermost of wounds.

*

Autumn on Mount La Verna. A gust of snow
Reminded us: Brother Donkey, the sack-cloth
Showing his ribs, at forty-three, worn through.

*

His body disciplined to stand ajar,
A threadbare sack, two sandals and a cord
Were all he had to guard it from the world.

Think of him as he must have been, the frail
And unregarded body that lay down
Nightly upon a grid in the dark cave:

A withered leaf that curls round its own form –
Though not resisting death, still on the tree,
Still of the world, simply by being there.

*

You who wake to the light of the high peaks,
Here is my darkness in this squalid cave.
But where do *you* lie down for your snow-dreams?

II
A Quotation

An angel here, there a tormented beast.

'The angel I can take; the beast, no.'

No choice: you must take both, or neither.

> *

Neither, then. Before long, the wound heals
And leaves in a nest of scars a crescent scar,
Unseen, till again your nakedness be shown.

III
As it Was

A Buddha's sleek tranquillity reflects
In a glazed wood veneer. Nearby is hung
An austere body on a crucifix,
Broken with pain, though sinuously young.

On a small chair the heap of clothes you've shed
Is like a crumpled statue. You, set free
From dressed propriety, stretch out on the bed
And draw me gently to your privacy.

No soul distinct from body, love from sex:
In sensuous lines, slight wrinkles, greying hair
I read a ghostly story, and the text
Has flourishes extravagant but spare.

You look at once so strong and vulnerable,
So shaped by fortune to a discipline,
I hardly dare to touch you. Yet I feel
Scar tissue in the smoothness of your skin.

IV
The Conversation

I think of this as of a conversation
That's run through the nine months we've spent apart,
You angry, me despairing; I remember

Stray phrases from your talk, which come to me
Like those quotations out of plays or poems
That bring delight in sorrow or console.

Yours, though, torment: with bitter truth, injustice
And all that beautiful intelligence
I may no longer love. I quote you quoting

From certain of the mystics that you read –
From Meister Eckhart or the *Dhammapada*
Or visionaries in whom eternal love

Leaves open wounds. Or else I quote from Shakespeare
And you respond: 'I've been re-reading him
And thinking how he dwells, as we have noticed,

On "nothing" – "all for nothing" and all that –
So that his nothing seems the source of all things.'
More often, though: 'You have betrayed my trust.

You've such good qualities: why do you spoil them?
Please keep away. Desire for you has gone.'
But my desire persists, an unhealed lesion

Scoured with your invective, 'nothing' then
Making a nothing out of dear remembrance,
Our pool of happiness too soon dried up,

Hope hopeless, and the future without meaning –
Except, perhaps, the kind of meaning found
In Shakespeare or a silent conversation.

V
Padre Pio
Francesco Forgione (1887–1968)

'That fucking whore-madonna…' and a fart
Of gut contempt, a man his body's functions.
They drove a spear into Francesco's heart.

Struck by his comrades. No, the Colonel said,
You could not make a man of him, the priest
No priest of him. So, without leave, he fled.

Bowels clenched, his inner force – from the assault
Contracting – shrank still further in, head split
Like continents adrift along a fault.

The Brothers took the burden on. But then
His inner world's deranged geography
Stabilised round an organising pain,

Which was the pain of Christ. Therefore not his.
He brooded as he celebrated Mass
And prayed, losing himself not to lose this.

Church hours passed. Pain, sweetened and perfumed,
Swirled through his body. Then a nameless love
Flushed at the portal of each sudden wound.

VI
Symmetry

'Lop-sided,' you once told me: more sensitive
On one side than the other, your right brain
More active than the left; but to attain
A self in balance was, you said, to live.

In a photograph your eyes speak, the right one
Of nurture and the force of it; the glaze
In the left, though, brings news of a cold place
It glimpsed once and will one day fix upon.

*

Monuments of the time of the Black Death
Might house two effigies: beauty above
In all its earthly splendour – like a meadow
Embroidered with the thousand flowers of May;

The other effigy, laid out beneath,
Foretells the flayed cadaver. You, my love,
Who walk with death, lie down beside his shadow,
The focused knowledge of your own decay.

VII
Spiritual Biography

*He is the Life and the End to which men must come; and He is the Door… We
must enter by this Door, by breaking through nature, and by the exercise of virtue
and humility…*

Johannes Tauler

In the first place, a medieval childhood:
in your father's hands
the huge key to the manor-house.
A ghost passed on the far side of the wall.
Later on,
hauntings of the spirit and hormones.
Then the retreat: 'where prayer has been valid',
who is it thrusts a knife into your sternum?
An angel, you would say. If ghosts, angels:
you have need of them.

You rise from that, as on the afternoon
you drove through a thunderstorm to a sick-bed,
your mother's, as she waited for the bolt

to strike into her life,
as simultaneously, on a road awash,
it stabbed into your heart.

To live your life was to walk with death.
                                    So when,
your child dead and husband gone,
you lay down on your couch as in your grave,
you fell into another space:
a passage, a garden at the end of it, a door
opening on light, a voice within it
that spoke in concert with an unseen throng,
their scent and music promise and presage.

VIII
Walled Garden

Hortus conclusus. The locked gates inspire
Trespassers: Casanova with young nuns…
The body vulnerable to its desire

Seeks out another who is vulnerable:
She, sealed in her apartness, broods within
Her body, which has served her as a wall

But, prone to ecstasy, might yet become
The means of access for a teeming world
That, touching her, would leave her chilled and numb.

It was always an illusion, that reserve.
There is no faith or hope that does not know
The odour of carnality, nor love

The neighbourhood of animals: lost sheep,
The ox and ass, the reek of stable straw,
The child at the swollen breast nodding asleep,

Who born in pain will end in pain, his bonds
Unbroken breaking him, his inwardness
Leaking into the world through his five wounds.

IX
The Second Day

The man of sorrows sleeps, his blood congealed:
His hair is clotted with the mud that stops
All orifices, and the tomb is sealed.

It is the day of rest and there is peace.
Despair brings certainty, a sober grief
And understanding. Argument may cease.

Yesterday was the earthquake and the storm,
Crowds, horror, iron hammered into flesh,
The rending of the veil, the foretold doom.

This is the second day. The text is mute.
I am Simon Peter, Thomas Didymus,
I contemplate my guilt, I mourn, I doubt.

Oh you, my love, my fair one, dew in your hair
And roses in your cheeks, you are gone now.
Love dies with you. This is the day of care.

Tomorrow, though, will be the crux of time:
I shall be John or Mary Magdalene
And I shall stand with spices at the tomb.

X
Piero's 'Resurrection' (1)

For some, pagan. The dawn dimly wakes,
Like a new season, raising the dead god,
We mortals sleeping on as the earth turns.

For you, Buddhist. The awakened one,
Pain and its seasons in his opened eyes,
Looks out beyond the torpor of desire.

For me, tragic. While no claggy earth
Clings to his body, there's the weight and drag
Of the numb sleep he cannot wish to leave.

Or Christian. Death known, the tide of light
Revisits these abandoned earthly shores,
Infusing them, as ghostliness the flesh.

XI
Piero's 'Resurrection' (2)

I dreamed we met in Borgo Sansepolcro
A second time, having again endured
The strange frustrations of the usual journey.

Such pleasure just to talk again! We strolled
In tears and laughter toward the city centre,
As if there'd been no breach. Just as before,

We stopped at an ordinary *trattoria* –
The meal we ate there far from commonplace –
Then on to the Palazzo Comunale

For Piero's *Resurrection*. There it stood,
Just as recalled, a layer of tinted plaster
That opened up the surface of a wall

In the long council chamber, giving substance
And bulk to its alert protagonist.
The figures in the foreground were all sleeping

Like us, held there before them in a dream,
But where the last time we'd been struck with silence,
Each sunk within a vision, now we spoke.

First you to me (both looking at the picture):
'Where have you been these nine months?' And then I:
'I have been buried by the weight of darkness,

My wounds all stopped with earth. And what of you?'
'I slept and underwent the full gestation,
And now I wake, reborn from my own sleep.'

The risen Christ then vanished from the painting;
I woke alone and saw the empty frame,
For he and you had filled the world with absence.

XII
Healer

A garden after nightfall rank with the smells
Of musk-rose, honeysuckle and mock-orange
Has eased its way into the front room

Of a terraced house the wrong side of the tracks.
From the kitchen you can hear an urgent sizzle,
Two boys are kicking a ball about in the yard

And a lone mother, wiping her busy hands,
Is taking on my pain. Intensely dark
And almost without highlights, her small eyes

Look into mine, their kindness inspires fear,
And talk of meridians and auric fields
Flutters weakly around their concentration –

Which is a concentration, you are sure,
That knows from the inside, works from the pain
That enters the world at birth. Therefore the hands

Held out above my wound radiate heat
And the room fills with a garden quite unknown
To the boys in the bare yard or the passers-by.

XIII
The Names of Flowers

Wild garlic, bugloss, toadflax – how you relished
The names of wayside flowers! It was as if,
In making words, your larynx, lips and tongue

A second time created the great world
And all its rich redundancy. We are
Sculptors of air and what we make is speech,

The given world as moulded to our needs
In our design. So coursing through our frames
The matter of our speech is briefly molten,

Soon to be set in grammar, prosody
And vocables. And so, in naming flowers,
Your beauty makes a beauty that knows theirs –

Teaches that what I name cannot be mine,
Who, living in my words as in the world,
Work to give utterance to that which is.

XIV
The Desert

You lead me to the desert. As we go,
You name the flowers we pass, gratuitous
In their abundance and variety.

But when the richness leaves us, you leave it,
And stone, sand, thorn and the stigmatic flesh
Become the matter of the universe.

Here is the proper place for meditation.
Where you confront the nothingness of things,
What space for someone added unto you?

And as for me, neither holy nor whole,
'My poetry is fragments, because I
Am fragments', yet the thought so often ours

Of being oned with God, your thought as mine,
Was brokenly revealed to me in all
The nothingness you brought upon my flesh.

The Need for Angels
Epilogue to 'Stigmata'

A blade
into your chest,
who drove it in?
An angel, I have said,
if there *are* angels.
Dante,
on the first
anniversary
of his grief,
drew an angel,
Beatrice
clear in his mind still.
Disturbed – 'Someone
was just with me,' he said –
he went on drawing, drawing
not yet writing.
You draw what you see,
but at times
not with the eye.
Dante, drawing,
knew her alive and,
knowing it,
wrote his poem.
Wounded,

writing it. For to see
without the eye
is to be pierced,
knife in the sternum.
Even so the angel
at La Verna
drove insight
into St Francis' side,
hands, feet.
So Pio. So Teresa.
Consummatum est
in the place of the skull.
You, walking with death,
know that place,
you who were there
in the cinema
looking away, sitting
that furnace of an afternoon
beside me but apart,
and it was then
I knew what I know.
Call it angel, call it love,
whatever:
the shaft
driven down into my body,
heart, bowels.
Too pure for me, you may be,
yet too wild – Eros
in each of us
diversely fierce –
too strong, too frail, too
holy not whole,
scourged by sorrow,
wounded by love –
but the shaft driven
into me, through me,
that tube of nothing,
fills with a long cry:
I, I love you, love you, love.
I, I love you, you.

REPORT FROM NOWHERE
& OTHER POEMS

(2006–2011)

I

To One who Accused Him of Writing Hate-mail

Not hate-mail: love-letters –
Read them again and see.
Love wounded is no angel: a wild beast,
Bellowing in distress.

Meditation

In your quiet room, the flux of candlelight:
You listen for things passing.
You shed the past like skin – I could believe
You hear the dry flakes fall.
And me, you squeeze me out of you
Like pus from a pustule.

To a Buddhist

Because desire is not to be desired,
Because the past must pass and death must die,
You do not find it difficult to accept
Your own acceptance of the end of love
As natural exhalation of drawn breath:

For me, the end of a companionship
So 'delicate and valuable' (your words)
The loss of it seems loss of everything
I have desired, so that I must accept
The past as nothing but the path to death.

The Nice and the Nasty

For the first time in months I find I can calmly survey the wreckage,
And I long for the Nice You back again, then suddenly recognise
That the Nice and Nasty Yous are separate parcels but one package.

The Language of Flowers
for M.V., with thanks

My emblem for her – delicate wild flower –
Rosa canina: Latin, the dog rose.

After the earthquake, 'Feminine,' said my friend.
'Think of the thorns. Not dog: *canina* – bitch.'

Message

I miss you. I hate you.
I hate being without you.

I want you. I love you.
I want to make love to you.

Bitch, bitch, bitch,
Why do you hurt so much?

To his Muse

Though our affair is over, it does seem
You can't stop visiting: here you are now,
Calling on me, what we say much the same –
Never my words though: yours, I don't know how.

II

Learning to Read
in memory of my father

You were the man who named the birds
And, as you did so, taught me words –

Words on the page, that pinion there
Articulations of the air,

Much as the birds mark out their ground
With brilliant instances of sound.

In the Conservatory

A bird's nest lined with leaves and moss
Kept here through the winter…
        Spring come, I find among leaf-mould
A brown mouse – its tail an unlikely flourish –
Modelling the letter 'C'
As if it stood for *Comfort*,
Though it lay there fixed and cold.

A Blue Tit's Egg

Freckled like the brow
Of a pale child – beaked open to reveal
A yellow fleck – no larger than my nail,
It was blown here on the wind.

Fledged or predated now,
The bird shrills in the thicket of my mind,
Unmindful how
Sturdy that first small crib was, yet how frail.

Gregoire, 60
for Gabriel

Jane Goodall met him in Brazzaville zoo – a living skeleton, every bone in his body visible, almost hairless from malnutrition. Born 1944. Believed to be the oldest chimpanzee in the world.
        Note from *James and Other Apes*. Photographs by James Mollison

Shakespeare – imagine him
Granted a further decade as God's spy.
He might have looked like this:
                                blanched white
The patchy beard, and parched the mottled skin.

Or Rembrandt, older still, and with an eye
As dim,
A will as faint,
A hand too frail to lift a brush and paint
His own nobility exposed to light.

Cinnabar Moth

What time is there
When a moth dies
For obsequies?
This cavalier,

Black barred with red,
Is ashes cast
On the blown air
As soon as dead.

Self-scattered dust
Enflames the eyes,
Which, though they mist,
Admit no tears.

A Curse

This is my curse
On the plump slinky slob of a Persian cat
That has moved in next door –
With never a rat
To trouble the neighbourhood. True,
Those collared doves that rehearse
Interminably their rebarbative coo
Are gone now, but before,
There were thrushes to sing, and a redbreast,
And vesperal blackbirds, and still
Quite often the terse
Repeated shrill
Of a blue-tit on guard near his boxed nest.
No more.
With no sound
But a car-alarm going off,
A shout, a beer-can crunched on the ground
And the flop of a flabby cat on my glass roof,
There is desolation in this urban place
And the neighbours, I should imagine, call it peace.

Gaudier-Brzeska in the Trenches
From his letters

The day's magnificent: the sky brushed clear,
Wind fresher, skylarks singing cheerfully…
Nothing I've yet heard has disturbed that choir –
Not the crude clamour, even, of the shells.

And in the woods at night the nightingales
Sing over us. They solemnly proclaim
Our conduct sacrilege and foolery.
I cannot but respect their high disdain.

A Farmhouse near Modena, c.1980
O magnum mysterium

In the dark, the grey
Carrara shafts, with their scrolled
capitals.
               A small boy
sprung out of nowhere
charges in, gloves flapping
about his wrists.
He stops short.

Hay in the mangers, straw
on the bricked ground,
                              and white
oxen parted by the shafts –
freed from the yoke, patient,
heads to the wall,
gilt traces
tingeing their soft horns.

The boy standing among them
awed, a farmhand
stoops into the corner to lift out
for his gaze
a mother hedgehog suckling her eight young,
pinkish tadpoles dangling
from her teats.

III

Remembering John Heath-Stubbs

Blínd Hómer: this is how he 'read':
Dragging each word up from the tap-roots,
Winching the world from well-spring to well-head,
Drawing speech into his mouth from under his boots.

Shakespeare
In Memoriam: E.E.I.

I must have been just eight – it was 1953 –
When in some parlour of my mind he pulled a chair out
Like a book from a packed shelf, then sat down and got going.
Fifty-eight years have passed and he hasn't finished talking
Nor I listening. My father was already dead,
My mother's now been dead for thirty years. Who else
Have I got to know like him, learnt more from, loved more freely?

Brook's 'Lear'
Aldwych Theatre, London, 1962

Cordelia dead, the King dead – oh, and Edmund.
His brother obeys the weight of the sad time:
He hoists the body and – houselights coming on –
Drags it upstage and off; at which time we,
As much as they, exit to numbed applause.

Afterwards, from the top deck of a bus,
I looked down at the great theatre of the world
With its forked animals
Acting and suffering, meeting and missing each other
Down there outside and, inside, in my thought.

In Hospital

The sun was going down and in low spirits
I turned on the hospital radio and heard
'Nobody Knows the Way I Feel this Morning'
By Sidney Bechet's New Orleans Feetwarmers.

The band stepped out in melancholy mode:
The blues. First the trombone, next the trumpet –
Muted, whining, over the steady tread.
Then not the clarinet, the soprano sax,

And Bechet – you could hear the brassy gleam –
Rode in on his fierce mount, its nostrils flared,
With gilded trophies slung across its neck,
To triumph over all adversity.

Fragment

                              And then
The end of consciousness begins to seem
Like a great woman, splayed across her bed
In shadow, curtains drawn against the day.
She summons you. She shows her darkness to you.
She draws you to her, whispering *My darling.*
Come home to me, my sweet one, stay with me.
Forget success and failure. Fuck, and sleep.

A Far-off Country

The country you have come to
Is strange and bewildering.
They do not speak your language,
The alphabet is different,
The road-signs unfamiliar.
The faces and the gestures
You find unreadable.
You are hungry, you are anxious,
But there's no one you can look to
For comfort or relief.

Sometimes there is beauty:
A light of lemon-colour
Through a tree's transparent leaves,
The polish of pink marble
On a bridge's parapet.
These lure you as a stranger might –
She leads you to a secret place
And once there, throat to knee
Without a word or gesture,
Unbuttons her thin dress.

It is that familiar strangeness:
Surprised, and yet expectant,
You know, yet do not know,
What you will now see.
It leaves you desolate.
You wander through vague streets,
A child without his mother
In a crush of giant strangers,
Eager to cry, and certain
She is not to be found.

Civitas
for Peter Carpenter

drove stakes in.
                    So that in good time
the stockade framed pictures of the wilderness.
                    So with all settlement.

I too keep watch.
I trample the nettles down which stand outside
the shored-up wall of Peterhouse on guard. For here,
as in 1280, Library and Hall secure,
the city of Cambridge ends
                    and the beautiful and fertile desolation
of the Fen Country begins:
willow and mare's tail, heron and lacewing,
ditch-water, tussock grass and the endless sky.

There are times when the rain
comes and comes again, and then the earth
turns to water, the pollarded willows stand
in water, paths disappear, and flocks
of waterbirds, their empire welling back,
honk, as if humankind had never been.

The poet Michael Longley, a gentle man
who knows too well those lovers of their race,
those neighbours who on Saturdays
plant bombs in civic centres – he told me
'I love looking at holes in roads,
when workmen dig up gas-pipes or whatever,
and you glimpse the soil buried for generations
and you see there can be no continuing city.'

Beneath tarmac, beyond city walls,
what have we lost or gained?
                    I remember
a day in the 1970s when a coach
taking me into London, toward sunset,

was stopped short
by a herd of cattle homeward bound, their herdsmen
driving them on across the strip of road
bisecting Wanstead Common. There it was:
suburb, and pasture, and cars in a slowed procession,
the unschooled drivers leaning on their horns,
and against a damson sky, in silhouette,
this scene from Samuel Palmer,
Arcadian not millenarian.

Those who in the name of life
expunge abortionists and vivisectionists
do not recover pastoral innocence.

Here behind Peterhouse is a patchwork –
outbuildings, car park, scrub and a new hotel.
I look for a thing I love:
above a blocked-in gateway, carved in stone,
a heraldic shield – in the top left-hand quarter
a martlet, poised for flight,
the beak ajar and pointing toward the sky, but barred
by the black letters ALF sprayed from a gun.

Report from Nowhere

It is not just the sex.
It is the reflection afterwards.

– as it might be in the fields, after haymaking, the sun
spread low along the horizon, shadows bold,
and they all troop off to the pub.
And the library. And the gallery.
And bed
with nightwork in the tangles of their minds.

POEMS WRITTEN FOR SIDNEY SUSSEX COLLEGE, CAMBRIDGE

(2009–10)

A Valedictory Ode

for Professor Dame Sandra Dawson
on the end of her tenure as Master of Sidney Sussex College, Cambridge

Wisdom must be a Lady, Saint Sophia,
And it is Dame Philosophy consoles.
Scholars and poets, sterile without Muses,
Are animated by their female souls.
And yet eight hundred years ago in Cambridge
Scholars were men – men, I repeat, not stones.
How did they live then? What queen bee inspired them,
And made them something more than bumbling drones?

And what of all the women who loved learning?
They founded Colleges: first Lady Clare,
Then Lady Pembroke, Lady Margaret Beaufort,
Two Queen Elizabeths, and here, yes, here
The Lady Frances Sidney, whose connections
Mastered the arts and learning – girls *and* boys –
And left an England rich with knowledge, beauty
And everything the civil life enjoys.

    Times change. Old hierarchies,
  Enlightened once, may now seem dark.
    Sidney, once patriarchal,
  Today is mastered by a matriarch.
We can imagine that the Lady Frances
  Looked down with pleasure, then,
When Sandra Dawson was acclaimed our Master
    Before those men!

    But, Master, time is stern:
Ten years have passed and you will have to leave us.
The fanfare ends. The Fellowship you've earned
Will make your stepping down a step less grievous.
In thanking you, we ask you to believe us –
You who've brought change – that we are changed in turn,
For we are scholars and, from you, we've learned.

2009

The Sidney Carol

Each year it comes round again:
      The aching chill,
      The ashen sky,
The sunset bleeding through the fen,
The freezing of our warm good will,
    The sense that things must die.
Each year it comes round again.

As every year, the shepherds squat
      On bleaching grass
      Around the fold.
Not asking if their life is what
Was always meant to come to pass
    Or why good things grow cold,
As every year, the shepherds squat.

Sure as the stars at evening rise,
      There are three kings
      Who year by year
Come seeking what will make them wise:
The new life which the winter brings,
    And which will now appear
Sure as the stars at evening rise.

In this bleak world what hope of joy?
      The ordeal of birth
      Has flecked with blood
A slight girl and her tiny boy.
They hear the song of peace on earth
    And trust in human good:
In this bleak world a hope of joy.

The year runs on and there is change:
      Not peace but war,
      My path is lost.
And yet the power of time is strange.
The winter child comes as before,

Like snowdrops in the frost.
The year runs on and there is change.

Once more, a choir of angels sings,
    As moonlight glows
      Within the ice.
The shepherds join them, and the kings.
Let us, too, join them, while it snows,
    To greet the new-born Christ.
Once more, a choir of angels sings.

2010

SELECTED POEMS FROM
THE HUNGARIAN

Translated with George Gömöri

JENŐ DSIDA (1907–1938)

Maundy Thursday

No connection. The train would be six hours
late, it was announced, and that Maundy Thursday
I sat for six hours in the airless dark
of the waiting room of Kocsárd's tiny station.
My soul was heavy and my body broken –
I felt like one who, on a secret journey,
sets out in darkness, summoned by the stars
on fateful earth, braving yet fleeing doom;
whose nerves are so alert that he can sense
enemies, far off, tracking him by stealth.
Outside the window, engines rumbled by
and dense smoke like the wing of a huge bat
brushed my face. I felt dull horror, gripped
by a deep bestial fear. I looked around:
it would have been so good to speak a little
to close friends, a few words to men you trust,
but there was only damp night, dark and chill,
Peter was now asleep, and James and John
asleep, and Matthew, all of them asleep…
Thick beads of cold sweat broke out on my brow
and then streamed down over my crumpled face.

MIKLÓS RADNÓTI (1909–1944)

Garden on Istenhegy

Summer has fallen asleep, it drones, and a grey veil
    Is drawn across the bright face of the day;
    A shadow vaults a bush, so my dog growls,
    His hackles bristling, then he runs away.

Shedding its petals one by one, a late flower stands
    Naked and half-alive. I hear the sound
    Of a withered apricot-bough crack overhead
    To sink of its own weight slowly to the ground.

Oh and the garden too prepares for sleep, its fruit
    Proffered to the heavy season of the dead.
    It is getting dark. Late too, a golden bee
    Is flying a death-circle around my head.

And as for you, young man, what mode of death awaits you?
    Will a shot hum like a beetle toward your heart,
    Or a loud bomb rend the earth so that your body
    Falls limb from limb, your young flesh torn apart?

In sleep the garden breathes. I question it in vain.
    Though still unanswered, I repeat it all.
    The noonday sun still flows in the ripe fruit
    Touched by the twilight chill of the dew fall.

20 July 1936

In the Margins of the Prophet Habakkuk

Whole cities
Were ablaze,
Villages
Crashed in smoke.
Be with me,
Stern prophet
Habakkuk!

The cinders
Have now cooled,
Black as coal,
But there's fire

In me still:
It will bite
And burn bright.

Gall to me
Is my food
And drink. From
Head to foot,
Black rage, coat
Me with soot.

1937

First Eclogue

Quippe ubi fas versum atque nefas: tot bella per orbem,
Tam multae scelerum facies…

Virgil

Shepherd:

It's long since we last met here. Did the song of the thrushes call you?

Poet:

I'm listening to the woods: there is such a din now spring's here!

Shepherd:

This isn't spring. The sky wants to fool us. Just look at this puddle:
Now it is smiling meekly, but at night when the frost congeals it
It'll bare its teeth! This is April: a fool's month to believe in.
Those little tulips there have been nipped in the bud by frost.
Why sad? Won't you sit down here on this stone beside me?

Poet:

It's not that I'm sad: I've grown so used to this terrible world
That sometimes I am not hurt by it – merely disgusted.

Shepherd:

What I'd heard is now certain. On the ridges of the wild Pyrenees
Red-hot cannon wrangle amid corpses stiff with blood,
And bears join with the soldiers as they flee.
In flocks, with knotted bundles, flee old folk, women and children,
Throwing themselves to the ground as death starts circling above,
And there are so many lying dead, they are left there, no one
                                                    removes them.
I think you knew Federico. Did he escape, ah tell me!

Poet:

He did not flee. They killed him. Two years ago in Granada.

Shepherd:

García Lorca is dead! And you are the first to tell me!
The news of war travels so fast, yet the poet
Can just disappear like that. Did Europe not mourn his death?

Poet:

It was not even noticed. At best, the wind in the pyre's ashes,
Groping, will find among them some broken line to remember.
This much is left, no more, to the curious who come after us.

Shepherd:

He did not flee. He died. But then where can a poet escape?
Nor did our belovèd Attila flee; he just said *No*
To the present state. And yet, who mourns him now he has fallen?
How do you live? Can your words still find an echo in these times?

Poet:

While cannon boom? Among smouldering ruins, deserted villages?
Still, I keep on writing and live in this frenzied world
As that oak over there: it knows it will be cut down and already
Is marked with a white cross, showing that there, tomorrow,
The woodcutter begins. Yet, as it waits, it puts forth a new leaf.
You are fortunate here: it's so still – few wolves come this way,
And as it is months since your master was here, you can often
Forget that the flock you tend belongs to somebody else.
God bless you. Time I get home, old night will have fallen upon me.
The butterfly dusk is fluttering, its wings shedding silver sift.

1938

Written in a Copy of 'Steep Path'

I am a poet and unnecessary,
Even when, wordless, I go murmuring
Ti-tum ti-tum. Who cares? Instead of me,
The nosy little devils sing.

And oh, believe me, do! Not without reason,
Prudent suspicion fans my face like breath:
I am a poet, good for the stake alone,
As witness to the truth,

Who knows that snow is white, that blood is red
And that the poppy's flower is red as well
With its fine, fuzzy stem green as the field,

Who knows that, in the end, he will be killed
Because he would not kill.

1 June 1939

Foaming Sky

The moon bobs on the sky's foam.
I wonder at being alive tonight.
Assiduous death keeps searching our dark time
And those he finds are all unearthly white.

Sometimes the year looks back, lets out a scream,
Looks back, then passes out appalled.
Again what a grim autumn's crouched behind me
And what a winter, numbed by pain and dulled!

The forest bled and, in the cycle
Of time, each hour would shed its blood.
The wind scrawled numbers, vast and dark,
On snow-drifts in the wood.

I have come to see both that and this.
I feel how heavily air weighs on the earth.
A warm silence, alive with rustling noises,
Envelops me – as before birth.

I stop under a tree whose leaves
Seethe with anger. Its branches creak.
One reaches down – to grasp my throat?
I am no coward, nor am I weak,

But tired. I hold my tongue. The branch
Gropes through my hair in silence, fearfully.
I know we ought to forget, but I
Never forget a single memory.

The moon founders in foam. Across the sky
A dark green track of poison has been driven.
I stand and roll myself a cigarette,
Slowly, carefully. I am living.

8 June 1940

Autumn Begins Restlessly

Restless the sun erupts, it's lapped today
By iron-grey, fire-fringed flags.
Its vapours stream down, and the floating light
Bites into louring fogs.

The clouds are ruffled. The smooth pane of the sky
Ripples in the wind, as the blue flies away.
The low flight of a swallow preparing to leave
Describes a screaming 'e' or 'a'.

Autumn begins restlessly: the leaves,
Dying in rust, are flailing up and down
And the sky's breath is cool.
The air gives off no warmth – nothing but smoke.
The sun no more than sighs today, and feebly.

A lizard scuttles on the great graveyard wall.
Autumn's ravening wasps,
Gorging on flesh, are buzzing rabidly.

Men on the banked earth
Of trenches sit and stare
At the deep fires of death.
The smell of heavy leaf-mould floats on the air.

Flame flies above the road –
Half light, half blood, it flares on the coming dark.
Brown leaves burning in the wind
Flutter, spark.

And clustered grapes weigh on the vine, the vine-shoots wilt.
Drily the stems of yellow flowers
Crackle, and seeds fall to the ground.

The meadow is swimming in the evening mist.
At length, the wild clattering sound
Of distant carts shakes from the trees
The few leaves that persist.

The landscape falls asleep.
Death, lovely in his white glide,
Settles on the countryside.
The sky cradles the garden.
Look: in your hair's an autumn leaf that's golden.
Above you, branches weep.

Ah but your flame must rise above death and autumn
And raise me, love, along with you.
Let the wise thing be to love me today –
Be wise and kiss me, hungry for dreams too.

Joyfully love me, do not leave me, fall
With me into the dark sky sleep creates.
Let's sleep. Out there, the thrush is well asleep.
The walnut, falling on fallen leaves piled deep,
Makes no harsh sound. And reason disintegrates.

10 October 1941

Night

The heart is asleep and, in the heart, anxiety.
The fly is asleep near the cobweb on the wall.
The house is quiet: not a scratch from a wakeful mouse.
The garden sleeps, the branch, the woodpecker in the trunk,
The beetle sleeps in the rose, the bee in the hive
And summer in the wheat-grains that are scattering.
Flame sleeps in the moon, too, cold medal on the sky.
Autumn is up and, to steal, goes stealthily by.

1 June 1942

Paris

Where the pavement of the Boulevard Saint Michel
Turns into Rue Cujas, there's a slight camber.
Oh time of youth, so wild and beautiful,
I've not forgotten you: my heart remembers
Like a mine-shaft your voice's resonance.
Our baker had his shop on Rue Monsieur le Prince.

And to the left, where the park trees show tall,
One tree was yellowing against the sky,
As if already it had glimpsed the fall.
Freedom, oh cherished nymph with the long thigh,
Are you still hiding in the twilight gold
Among the veiling trees, just as you were of old?

Summer was like an army marching in
To drumbeats, sweating, raising dust on the road.
A cool mist followed in its tracks, and then
To either side of it a fragrance flowed.
Noon was still summertime; come afternoon,
Sweet autumn visited behind a front of rain.

In those days I enjoyed a life unbound
As a child does, yet I was one who'd know,
Like an old pedant, that the earth was round.
I was green still, but with a beard like snow.
I wandered freely. Whom would it concern?
Then going underground, I felt the deep fires burn.

Where are you now, O stations of time past:
CHATELET – CITE – ST MICH' and ODEON?
Then DENFERT-ROCHEREAU – like a name cursed.
The map that flowered on the stained wall is gone.
I shout: Where are you? And I strain to hear,
As if the sweat and ozone were roaring in my ear.

And then the nights! Those wanderings by night
From the outskirts toward the Quartier!
Will dawn ever again with its strange light
Pierce through the dull sky as a soft grey,
As when, from poetising, drunk in the head,
I undressed half-asleep and fell into my bed.

If only I had the strength just to return
And skip the headlong current of my fate!
The cat from the cheap, smelly restaurant
Downstairs would go up on the roof to mate.
The noise it made! Will I, just once again,
Hear that? For then I learned in what a din
Noah, so long ago, floated beneath the moon.

14 August 1943

O Ancient Prisons

O peace of ancient prisons, beautiful
    Outmoded suffering, the heroic stance
Sublimely struck, the poet's death, and all
    Such measured speech as finds an audience –
How far away they are. Whoever dares
    Even move, steps in the void. A foggy blur.
Reality, like damaged earthenware,
    Bulges and waits for the one thing to occur:
To be reduced to shards and rottenness.
    How will it be for him who for the time
    He lives – allowed to – speaks in measured rhyme
And teaches judgement of whatever *is*?

    And would teach still. But all things fall apart.
    He sits and stares: is utterly inert.

27 March 1944

Eighth Eclogue

Poet:

Hail! How well you endure this rugged mountain walk,
Fine old man. Is it that wings lift you or enemies hunt you?
Wings bear you, passion drives you, lightning flares in your eyes.
Hail, venerable elder! You are one, I now perceive,
Of the ireful prophets of old – but tell me, which of their number?

Prophet:

Which am I? I am Nahum the Elkoshite. It was I
Who thundered against the concupiscent city of Nineveh, I
Who declaimed the word of the Lord, his brimming vessel of anger.

Poet:

I know your ancient fury – your writings have been preserved.

Prophet:

They have. But more than of old, today, sin multiplies,
Yet even today there is no one who knows what the Lord's end is.
For the Lord said he would cause the abundant rivers to dry up,
Bashan to languish, and Carmel, and Lebanon's flower to wither,
The mountains would quake – all things would be consumed in fire.
And all this has befallen.

Poet:

                    To the slaughter nations scramble.
And the soul of man is stripped bare, even as Nineveh.
What use had admonitions? And the savage ravening locusts
In their green clouds, what effect? Of all beasts man is the basest.
Here, tiny babes are dashed against walls and, over there,
The church tower is a torch, the house an oven roasting
Its own people. Whole factories fly up in their smoke.
The street runs mad with people on fire, then swoons with a wail,
The vast bomb-bays disgorge, the great clamps loose their burdens

And the dead lie there, shrivelled, spattering city squares
Like a herd's dung on the pasture: everything, once again,
Has happened as you foretold. What brings you back here, tell me,
To earth from ancient cloud-swirl?

Prophet:

          Wrath: that man as ever
Is an orphan again among the hosts of the seeming-human,
The heathen. And I wish again to see the strongholds of sin
Fall – wish to bear witness for the ages yet to come.

Poet:

You have already done so. The Lord spoke through you long ago:
Cried woe to the fortress filled with the spoils of war – with bastions
Built of cadavers! But tell me, can it be so that fury
Has survived in you these millennia – with divine, unquenchable blaze?

Prophet:

There was a time when the Lord touched my unclean lips
As he did the sage Isaiah's. With his ember hovering over me
God probed my heart. The coal was a live coal and red-hot –
An angel held it with tongs and 'Look, here am I: let me
Also be called upon to preach thy word' I cried after him.
And once a man has been sent by the Lord, he has no age,
He has no peace. The coal, angelic, burns on in his lips.
And what is a thousand years to the Lord? A mayfly time!

Poet:

How young you are, father! I envy you. What is my own brief time
To your awesome age? Even these few fleeting moments
Are wearing me down – like a round stone in a wild stream.

Prophet:

So you may think. But I know your new poems. Wrath nurtures you.
The poet's wrath, like the prophet's – it is food and drink

To the people. Whoever would may live on it until
The coming of the kingdom that young disciple promised,
The young rabbi whose life fulfilled our words and the law.
Come with me to preach that already the hour is at hand,
The kingdom about to be born. 'What,' I asked before,
'Is the Lord's end?' Lo, it is that kingdom. Come let us go:
Gather the people together. Bring your wife. Cut staffs.
Staffs for the wanderer are good companions. Look:
That one, let me have that one: I like the gnarled ones better.

Lager Heideman
23 August 1944

Forced March

A fool he is who, collapsed,   rises and walks again,
Ankles and knees moving   alone, like wandering pain,
Yet he, as if wings uplifted him,   sets out on his way,
And in vain the ditch calls him   back, who dare not stay.
And if asked why not, he might answer   – without leaving his path –
That his wife was awaiting him,   and a saner, more beautiful death.
Poor fool! He's out of his mind: now, for a long time,
Only scorched winds have whirled   over the houses at home,
The wall has been laid low,   the plum-tree is broken there,
The night of our native hearth   flutters, thick with fear.
Oh if only I could believe   that everything of worth
Were not just in my heart –   that I still had a home on earth.
If only I had! As before,   jam made fresh from the plum
Would cool on the old verandah,   in peace the bee would hum,
And an end-of-summer stillness   would bask in the drowsy garden,
Naked among the leaves   would sway the fruit-trees' burden,
And there would be Fanni waiting   blonde, by the russet hedgerow,
As the slow morning painted   slow shadow over shadow…
Could it perhaps still be?   The moon tonight's so round!
Don't leave me, friend, shout at me: I'll get up off the ground!

15 September 1944

Postcards

I

From Bulgaria, wild and swollen, the noise of cannon rolls;
It booms against the ridge, then hesitates, and falls.
Men, animals, carts, thoughts pile up as they fly;
The road rears back and whinnies, maned is the racing sky.
But you in this shifting chaos are what in me is constant:
In my soul's depth forever, you shine – you are as silent
And motionless as an angel who marvels at destruction,
Or a beetle burrowing in a hollow tree's corruption.

In the mountains
30 August 1944

II

No more than six or seven miles away
Haystacks and houses flare;
There, on the meadow's verges, peasants crouch,
Pipe-smoking, dumb with fear.
Here still, where the tiny shepherdess steps in,
Ripples on the lake spread;
A flock of ruffled sheep bend over it
And drink the clouds they tread.

Cservenka
6 October 1944

III

Blood-red, the spittle drools from the oxen's mouths,
The men stooping to urinate pass blood,
The squad stands bunched in groups whose reek disgusts.
And loathsome death blows overhead in gusts.

Mohács
24 October 1944

IV

I fell beside him. His body, which was taut
As a cord is when it snaps, spun as I fell.
Shot in the neck. 'This is how you will end,'
I whispered to myself. 'Keep lying still.
Now, patience is flowering into death.'
'*Der springt noch auf,*' said someone over me.
Blood on my ears was drying, caked with earth.

Szentkirályszabadja
31 October 1944

ISTVÁN VAS (1910–1991)

Romanus Sum

Romanus sum – and I held my hand in fire;
Through twenty years it has burnt me to the bone.
I played the part of Mucius Scaevola
Before what would, though yet unborn, be Rome.

And suddenly it was here. All that the past
Has spewed ferments between its malformed walls.
Rome has not yet been built but in its place,
Bloated with lies, a new Byzantium swells.

And the crucifix is debased to a gilded bauble
And the flames of Pentecost lap a martyr's stake.
It was such a waste to have burnt one's living flesh
For a stillborn City's sake.

c.1952

JÁNOS PILINSZKY (1921–1981)

Harbach 1944

I keep on seeing them: a shaft
rears and the moon is full –
there are men harnessed to the shaft.
It's a huge cart they pull.

They are dragging a massive wagon,
which grows as the night does,
their bodies split between the claims
of hunger, trembling, dust.

They bear the road, the horizon,
the beet fields shivering,
but only feel the burdening land,
the weight of everything.

Their neighbours' fallen flesh
seems stuck into their own,
as in each other's tracks they sway,
to living layers grown.

Villages keep clear of them
and gates avoid their feet.
The distances approaching them
falter and retreat.

Staggering, they wade knee-deep
in the dark, muffled sound
of clattering clogs, as if unseen
leaves carpeted the ground.

Silence accepts their frames. Each face
is dipped in height, as if
straining for the scent of troughs
in the sky far off.

And like a cattle-yard prepared
for the herded beasts outside –
its gates flung open violently –
death, for them, gapes wide.

The French Prisoner

If only I could forget him, the Frenchman
I saw outside our quarters, creeping round
near daybreak in that density of garden
as if he'd almost grown into the ground.
He was just looking back, peering about him
to check that he was safe here and alone:
once he was sure, his plunder was all his!
Whatever chanced, he'd not be moving on.

He was already eating. He was wolfing
a pilfered turnip hidden in his rags.
Eating raw cattle feed. But he'd no sooner
swallowed a mouthful than it made him gag;
and the sweet food encountered on his tongue

delight and then disgust, as it might be
the unhappy and the happy, meeting in
their bodies' all-consuming ecstasy.

Only forget that body … Shoulder blades
trembling, and a hand all skin and bone,
the palm cramming his mouth in such a way
that it too seemed to feed in clinging on.
And then the furious and desperate shame
of organs galled with one another, forced
to tear from one another what should bind them
together in community at last.

The way his clumsy feet had been left out
of all that gibbering bestial joy; and how
they stood splayed out and paralysed beneath
the body's torture and fierce rapture now.
And his look too – if I could forget that!
Retching, he went on gobbling as if driven
on and on, just to eat, no matter what,
anything, this or that, himself even.

Why go on? It turned out that he'd escaped
from the prison camp nearby – guards came for him.
I wander, as I did then in that garden,
among my garden shadows here at home.
'If only I could forget him, the Frenchman' –
I'm looking through my notes, I read one out,
and from my ears, my eyes, my mouth, the seething
memory boils over in his shout:

'I'm hungry!' And immediately I feel
the undying hunger which this wretched creature
has long since ceased to feel, for which there is
no mitigating nourishment in nature.
He feeds on me. More and more hungrily!
And I'm less and less sufficient, for my part.
Now he, who would have been contented once
with any kind of food, demands my heart.

The Passion at Ravensbrück

One steps clear of the others, stands
in a block of silence, still.
The prison garb, the convict's scalp
blink like an old film-reel.

Fearful to be a self alone:
the pores are visible,
with everything around so huge
and everything so small.

And that was it. As for the rest –
for the rest, without a sound,
simply forgetting to cry out,
the body hit the ground.

Introitus

Who will open the book which is now closed?
Who make the first cut into unbroken time?
Turning the pages over, dawn to dawn,
lifting the pages up, casting them down?

Who of us dares reach into the furnace
of the not-yet-known? Who furthermore would dare
search through the dense leaves of the sealed book?
And who is there to do so with hands bare?

And who of us is not afraid? Who'd not be
when God himself has shut his eyes, and when
the angels all fall down before his face,
and when his creatures darken, every one?

The Lamb, alone of us, is not afraid,
he only, who was slain: the Lamb who (look!)
now comes clattering over the glass sea
and mounts the throne. And then, opens the book.

Van Gogh's Prayer

A battle lost in the cornfields
and in the sky a victory.
Birds, the sun and birds again.
By night, what will be left of me?

By night, only a row of lamps,
a wall of yellow clay that shines,
and down the garden, through the trees,
like candles in a row, the panes;

there I dwelt once and dwell no longer –
I can't live where I once lived, though
the roof there used to cover me.
Lord, you covered me long ago.

GYÖRGY GÖMÖRI (b. 1934)

Fake Semblances of Odysseus

Fake semblances of Odysseus, we wander over the planet
while at home our Penelopes, formerly smiling,
have suddenly gone serious
and taken to the weaving of winding-sheets…
It's winter now, our galleys are burdened with frost,
an evil north wind wails over grey seas,
the stars, moreover, are so inhumanly abstract.

We did not stay behind with the lotus-eaters,
were not broken apart by Charybdis and Scylla,
but *are* consumed with the consciousness
that, look, the struggle is not yet over
and at home the suddenly serious Penelopes
are weaving shrouds, funereal winding-sheets.

Famous Achaeans, what was the worth of your empty chatter?
Did you make sacrifices to Poseidon,
the dull-brained but mighty? Have you ever been able
to challenge him with brave deeds? Did you ever do so?
You have given us food, but otherwise there is nothing
but nimble words to lament or juggle with –
that's all you've been able to do,
famous Achaeans.

Fake semblances of Odysseus, we wander over the planet.
The sea is weaving a winding-sheet of our sighs.
The past is sunken in fog, thick fog hides Ithaca's fate.

Oxford, 1956

Letter from a Declining Empire

Ever more frightening, ever more rapacious,
barbarian incursions are troubling
the Empire of Autumn.
And galloping on, the northerly wind
screeches through cloud-crevices, shears off
leafy crowns, tears down
beech-tree robes the colour of sealing-wax,
shedding their heavy blood,
cracking its whip at defencelessly shuddering maples –
and how the gold coins keep falling!
Down threadbare avenues, past gap-toothed palings
the raider goes clattering by; he throws
a firebrand into a chestnut-tree, and whoosh!
leaves whirl and fly up into
an air-woven hoop of flame. There's no one by
to save the treasures, the infidel
can pillage unhindered, there are now
only scattered watchtowers of silver fir left standing.
And still the conquest is incomplete. It's in vain

that the frost-riders patrol down by the river, in vain
that the Khan exacts his ransom from the milder
October colours, from sky-blue and green;
the survivors learn how to live. As naked
as cornstalks rent and torn, and with earth's bitterness.
Once the marauders have cleared off, their savage
symbols will also melt and trickle down the gardens – and then
all of a sudden the new
but eternal year will rise and raise with sunshine a still more
                                        beautiful empire.

DOMOKOS SZILÁGYI (1938–1976)

Job
A Statue by Meštrović

All skin and bone, an old Jew, fit to die,
howls from this dust-heap earth at the cold sky.
According to His will, the Lord up there
has used and done for him: now Father dear,
now wicked goblin – whether bad or good
depends entirely on his changing mood.
All skin and bone, an old Jew, fit to die,
howls from this dust-heap earth at the cold sky:
'Naked, O Lord, orphaned and poor I've stayed
that You might never lose the bet You made
with Satan – not on my account – that he
'd go green to witness such deep loyalty.
Whatever by caprice You chose to take –
three daughters, seven sons – I for Your sake
have laid before You, Lord, with my livestock –
asses, camels, every herd and flock.
But this is all mere air – nothing to me.
I ask no greater favour than to be
a beggar, Lord. Let me be plagued with lice,

let rampant sores consume me, and may this
seem so much more than a good job well done
that in the end You'll say: "Good Job, good son,
enough: there's no one of more trust and worth
than My true servant Job throughout the earth.
His flock is scattered, every beast is dead,
there is a dust-heap where he laid his head
and poverty is now his bedfellow,
making him of all beggars there below
the wretchedest … Come, angel, the good Lord
must see His Job's prosperity restored –
which Job once lost in answer to My voice.
Now he will get three girls and seven boys,
a burgeoning harvest and a mighty herd,
long life and power with it. This is My word.'"
Job then says: 'Lord, rejoice, as you may well,
But not to wipe out all that once befell.
One suffered. Was that nothing? It can't be so.
What does it matter if, adoring You,
I live four generations, always well
acquainted with Your mercy, and of all
those days no day is spent in weeds and dung?
But however much I am, by old or young,
loved and respected, no, no one can be –
not even You – lord over memory.
For during sleepless nights, my grandchildren
will still remember as they toss and turn,
and feverish with horror they will cry
howling from beds of flame at the cold sky.'

GYÖRGY PETRI (1943–2000)

You are Knackered, my Catullus

You are knackered, my Catullus, you wake with a skull
heavy as stone, your feet tight bags of water.
As for your mirror, better not look. Not all of Rome's
most refined balsams would restore your slack and pallid skin.
And your teeth, too, teeth that were once so white! –
that's how a city wall, once ruined, turns to decay.
Where now are the days of 'ready for nine embraces in one go'?
Your used-up body, the yawning silent sum of all of this,
does not tell to what extent the causes of this effect
were a great passion, exemplary for centuries,
and to what extent ceaseless, omnivorous greed –
how much due to the poison of deliciously high living
and how much to the stewed gut-rot of low taverns.

Stairs

Who was it invented
circumscribed fall
– stairs,
which tame height, the frozen
perpendicular melted
down to degrees; and –
the cunning of the solution –
showed wingless man
the modest trick
of the detour, when he'd
try to jump
in vain after his glance?

Now Only

now only the filthy pattering of rain
now only heavy coats and squelching shoes
now only the din of steamed-up cheap cafés
now only trodden sawdust on the stone

now only mouldy buns in cellophane
now streetlights decomposing in thin fog
the advice given by a friendly cop
the last drink bought with the last of the small change

now only the tram island's desolation
now only the variable course of the night wind
rushing through a town of alleys to no end

now only the unfinished excavations
the night's prospecting-hole its weeds and thorns
now only shivering now only yawns

Gratitude

The idiotic silence of state holidays
is no different
from that of Catholic Sundays.
People in collective idleness
are even more repellent
than they are when purpose has harnessed them.

Today I will not
in my old ungrateful way
let gratuitous love decay in me.
In the vacuum of streets
what helps me to escape
is the memory of your face and thighs,
your warmth,
the fish-death smell of your groin.

You looked for a bathroom in vain.
The bed was uncomfortable
like a roof ridge.
The mattress smelt of insecticide,
the new scent of your body mingling with it.

I woke to a cannonade.
(A round number of years ago
something happened.) You were still asleep.
Your glasses, your patent leather bag
on the floor, your dress on the window-catch
hung inside out – so practical.

One strap of your black slip
had slithered off.
And a gentle light was wavering
on the downs of your neck, on your collar-bones,
as the cannon went on booming

and on a spring poking through
the armchair's cover
fine dust was trembling.

To Be Said Over and Over Again

I glance down at my shoe and – there's the lace!
This can't be gaol then, can it, in that case.

Electra

What *they* think is it's the twists and turns of politics
that keep me ticking; they think it's Mycenae's fate.
Take my little sister, cute sensitive Chrysothemis –
to me the poor thing attributes a surfeit of moral passion,
believing I'm unable to get over

the issue of our father's twisted death.
What do I care for that gross geyser of spunk
who murdered his own daughter! The steps into the bath
were slippery with soap – and the axe's edge too sharp.
But that this Aegisthus, with his trainee barber's face,
should swagger about and hold sway in this wretched town,
and that our mother, like a venerably double-chinned old whore,
should dally with him simpering – everybody pretending
not to see, not to know anything. Even the Sun
glitters above, like a lie forged of pure gold,
the false coin of the gods!
Well, that's why! That's why! Because of disgust, because it all sticks
$\qquad\qquad\qquad\qquad\qquad\qquad\qquad\qquad$ in my craw,
revenge has become my dream and my daily bread.
And this revulsion is stronger than the gods.
I already see how mould is creeping across Mycenae,
which is the mould of madness and destruction.

To Imre Nagy

You were impersonal, too, like the other leaders,
bespectacled, sober-suited; your voice lacked
sonority, for you didn't know quite what to say

on the spur of the moment to the gathered multitude. This urgency
was precisely the thing you found strange. I heard you,
old man in pince-nez, and was disappointed,
not yet to know

of the concrete yard where most likely the prosecutor
rattled off the sentence, or
of the rope's rough bruising, the ultimate shame.

Who can say what you might have said
from that balcony? Butchered opportunities
never return. Neither prison nor death
can re-sharpen the cutting edge of the moment

once it's been chipped. What we can do, though, is remember
the hurt, reluctant, hesitant man
who nonetheless soaked up
anger, delusion
and a whole nation's blind hope,

when the town woke to gunfire
that blew it apart.

Daydreams

Into destruction I would bring
an order whole and classical.
Hope for the good? Out of the question.
Let me die invisible.

Sors bona nihil aliud. To
whoever digs my bones I send
a message: which is, Look how all
God's picture-images must end.

And no there cannot be a heaven,
or else there oughtn't to be one
for, if there were, this plague of love
would still (come what may) go on.

Nor do I want the obverse – hell –
though of that I've had, will have, my bit
(planks beneath the chainsaw wail).

For anything unready, yet
ready too, I lie in the sun:
let the redeeming nowhere come.

A Recognition

1

The weather-beaten captain of a small riverboat,
I used to navigate history's local route.
I have come ashore now. Not through desert, but duty.
Here I am and the whole thing's beyond me.

2

The epoch expired like a monstrous predator.
My favourite toy's been snatched.

What a Shame

What a shame to die this way,
just now, when things could be OK –
though even like this it's not *too* bad:
I'll go quietly, almost glad
to mix with water, leaf-mould, clay,
thawed snow, showers of a summer's day
and autumn leaves that smell like booze.
The quiet hill waits for my repose –
and say, Will the muses of my song
rest there beside me before long?
(I'd go there right away, but who
will care for Mari if I do?
And who will bring her flowers home
when I am gnawed at by the worm?)

A Smile

I'm going to die, and pretty soon too.
This makes me slightly dizzy – not unlike
what I felt as a lad when I'd just started smoking:
the first few drags I'd take at a cigarette
on the balcony in the morning. It's long since passed,
of course, as so many other things have.
Now, though, of all those things, just one has stayed
and (God be thanked for it!) it is still there.
The keen, inquisitive hunger of the eye,
the pleasure of looking – everything seen pure joy,
each thing in its own way
equally beautiful – clear honey, and tar,
and the intertwining pipes in a boiler room
wrapped round with fibre-glass and silver foil.
Or the turquoise silence of a mountain lake
amid blue pines in glass-cold air. Or on the asphalt,
a fag-packet chucked away, that's aimlessly,
noisily, flapping about at the will
of the changing wind. The smile
of a small, pale, old woman with sunken gums,
a teardrop like yellow resin in the corner of her eye,
as also the hint of a double chin
on a firm-fleshed young girl flashing white teeth
and doing so, perhaps, just a little too much.
But this doesn't matter: flaws
are the source and spice of beauty. Then, too,
the legs of working women embroidered with varicose veins
and a fishwife at the market, her frozen, purple hands
slimy with catfish mucus and carp blood…
For the angel is in the detail.

Without

It's hard to imagine
the world without me.
But who says
I have to?

Besides, I can:
a bowl full of cream
and no cat.

ANNA T. SZABÓ (b. 1972)

The Labour Ward

I walk along the corridor, my tears
falling on the lino floor. The hormones.
In pain, the child inside me moves about.
The womb like a clenched fist pushes him,
squeezes him out.

Borne forward on a wave of mighty forces
I clutch at tables and chairs.
Pain stretches me, spins me, makes me twist.
Let it: I won't resist.

                    *

Animals whelp in their dens. Women, though,
must suffer together. In the labour ward,
babies – through the dark straits,
in mortal strife, to the sound
of a long, drawn-out, polyphonic wail –
inch forward.

*

Pain's like a demon, it seeks an object,
seizes you, takes you over, gets to be part of you.
Already you are it:
pulsating and endless – and over in two minutes.

And again it bears you, like water, like the wind.
The language it speaks is barbarous, primeval.
It pours from your mouth, an immemorial wail,
an otherworldly keening.

You cry for him, as well as for his seed,
as your pain pushes him into the world
to feed the thronging demons –
here they are now,
at your gate, waiting.

*

Bare little slippery snail, do come out.
Your home, it is wailing and tossed all about.
From its door there is pouring a rush of red flame.
Come on out, little snail, come slither in slime!

*

Oh child, you dead weight, you hot iron, you stone,
come forth now, I beg you, creep out on your own.
You stretch me apart, I am stretching you too.
Slither out now, my faceless one, you!

*

It pulls you. Thrusts. Stretches. You can do nothing.
Seven hours. It pulls you apart. Keep breathing.

To pray? To curse? Neither one, no.
There's too much pain. It's too alien now.

Don't fight against it, just let go.
This suffering, it isn't you.
Yet this hour is yours alone:
nobody but you can bear
your child, your son.

I was born for this. I expected it.
The gift of a child – that it might move
in the body's writhing basket.
From the contracting inner space
I hear, on the monitor, his heartbeat.
It pulsates quickly, in fits and starts:
pushing with his head, lunging forward,
widening the exit.

I struggle, panting. I breathe
with my whole body, an air spout.
Oxygen flooding in,
black nothingness floating out.

It hurts, to start with, yet you manage.
It's bearable... But then it grows,
flows surging through your consciousness,
engrossing everything. It turns
a woman to a wolf that howls.
Her fist clenched on the bedstead,
she's now in water to her brows,
crying for help, from under water
shouting, screaming silently,
as if her time had all run out –
but now the pain comes in a wave,

rolls over, falls upon itself
and flees – where? Far away – who knows?
A moment's breath, the grace of a pause.

*

Good that I'm not alone.
I have support, I'm helped.
My blood is wiped away.
My hands are held, caressed.

There, amid black waves,
I clutch at, gulp the air.
Not yet, not yet, I can't.
I can hold, just can't push.

Scared, shipwrecked, on the raft
of my body tossed about,
he clings to the slippery plank:
my child. My baby boy.

*

The pain's no longer physical. I am
a basin it has carved out of the earth.
Just movement: can't be bounded by one place.
It is a raging, elemental force.

*

Thrusting, he bangs on the door
of the wide world outside, full of air:
a child fighting off destruction
with all his force and fear.

His large head and bony bulk
will pass through the eye of a needle, but,
once they are through, there he just lies –
terrified, fists and eyes
still shut.

She Leaves Me

She betrays me, she leaves me.
She pushes me out of herself, and leaves me.
She offers herself to feed on, and leaves me.
She rocks me and she leaves me.
Wipes my bottom, combs my hair,
caresses the soles of my feet, but leaves me.
My nose drinks in her fragrance, how she hugs me:
she says, 'I'll never leave you!' And she leaves me.
She tricks me: smiling, whispers 'Don't be scared!'
I *am* scared, and I'm cold, and yet she leaves me.
She lies down on the bed with me at evening,
but soon enough she slips away and leaves me.
She is so big, so warm, alive, a nest,
she kisses me, and hums to me, and leaves me.
She presses sweets into my open palms
and 'There you are, eat now,' she says, and leaves me.
I cry and howl and press her frame to mine;
I can hold her, hit her too; and yet she leaves me.
She shuts the door, does not look back at all,
I'm nothing when she leaves me.
I wait for her return, a cringing cur:
she then arrives and strokes me, and she leaves me.
I need her – it is death to live without her –
she picks me up to warm me, and she leaves me.
Her arms make up a cage, her lap's a house;
I'd love to go back in there, but she leaves me.
I come to one conclusion: I'm not her:
a stranger, she's a stranger, and she leaves me.

Out there's the world, where someone will be waiting!
For you, there will be someone there to leave.
Don't look back. Shut the door. You know
how easy it is to wait, how hard to go.
Some you'll grieve, others will deceive you,
some will wait, others fear your lack,
and some there'll always be who don't come back:
they give you life, but then they die and leave you.

OTHER TRANSLATIONS

'Odi et Amo'

I hate and love. You may well ask why so.
I cannot say; the pain is what I know.

FROM THE ITALIAN OF ST FRANCIS OF ASSISI (1181?–1226)

Canticle of the Sun

O my good Lord, almighty and most high,
Thine are the praise, the honour and the glory
And thereto every blessing.
To thee alone are they due, thee they become,
And worthy is no man to give tongue to thy name.

Praise be to thee, my Lord, with all thou'st made,
And in especial Master Sun, our brother,
Who bringeth day, by whom thou givest light.
Comely he is and bright, of a great shining,
And in thy likeness doth he shape his meaning.

Praise be, my Lord, in Sister Moon and the stars:
In heaven thou mad'st them, costly and bright and fair.

Praise be, my Lord, in Brother Wind and the air
In cloudy and clear sky and in all weathers:
By him thou dost sustain life in thy creatures.

Praise be, my Lord, also in Sister Water,
Who serveth all, lowly and precious and pure.

Praise be, my Lord, also in Brother Fire,
Whereby thou dost illumine the night well,
And he is handsome and jocund, strong and hale.

Praise be, my Lord, in our sister, Mother Earth,
Who nurtureth and governeth us all.
So many kinds of fruit she bringeth forth
With grass and with bright flowers.

Praise be, my Lord, in them who for thy love
Forgive and bear much pain and tribulation.
Blest who bear such in peace, most high,
For by thy hand shall they be crowned in heaven.

Praise be, my Lord, in Sister Death.
None living can escape her.
Woe to all them that die in mortal sin.
Blest whom she findeth in thy holy will –
The second death shall not harm them.

Give thanks to my Lord, bless him, sing his praise,
And serve him humbly all your days.

FROM THE ITALIAN OF DANTE ALIGHIERI (1265–1321)

Sestina

I have come now to the long arc of shadow
And the short day, alas, and where the hills
Whiten, the colour gone from the old grass;
Yet my desire is constant in its green,
It has so taken root in the hard stone
That speaks and hears as if it were a woman.

Similarly this miracle of woman
Stays frozen like the deep snow left in shadow:
For she is no more moved than is a stone
By the sweet season – that which warms the hills
Turning the whiteness of them into green
And decking them in wild flowers, herbs and grass.

When her hair is garlanded with woven grass,
She draws the mind away from other women:
She braids the rippling yellow with the green
So beautifully, Love lingers in their shadow –
Love, who confines me here between low hills
More stringently than mortar binding stone.

Her beauty holds more power than precious stones
And nothing remedies – not herb or grass –
The hurt she gives: so over plain and hill
I have fled, my one need to escape that woman,
But from her eyes' clear light have found no shadow
By mountain, wall or leafage dense with green.

There was a time I saw her dressed in green
In such a way she could have made a stone
Feel the great love I bear her very shadow;
I desired her, therefore, in a field of grass –
As much in love as ever any woman
Has been – and ringed about by lofty hills.

But rivers will flow back and climb their hills
Before this wood, which is both damp and green,
Will at my touch catch fire – as fair women
Are known to do; and I would sleep on stone
My whole life long and go feeding on grass
Only to see where her dress casts a shadow.

Whenever the hills cast their blackest shadow,
With lovely green she makes it, this young woman,
Vanish, as stones are hidden in the grass.

Dante to Love's Faithful
from the 'Vita Nuova'

To every noble heart these words may move,
Each captive soul that looks into their theme,
I send – to learn how you interpret them –
This greeting in your Lord's name, which is Love.

The stars were shining clear, the starlit hour
Then on the point of passing was the third,
When suddenly Love in his own form appeared;
And to recall that form grips me with horror.

Happy Love seemed: I saw that in one hand
He clutched my heart, while she I love was laid
Across his arms, wrapped in a cloth and sleeping.

Then when he woke her, though she was afraid
He humbly fed the heart to her, which burned:
And as he went away, I saw him weeping.

FROM THE ITALIAN OF GUIDO CAVALCANTI (c.1255–1300)

Cavalcanti's Reply*

All the nobility men may know on earth,
The joy, the good, it seems to me you saw;
That noble Lord was proving you, whose law
Commands the world of honourable worth.

For where he lives, harsh dreariness must die;
With reason he holds sway in the mind's keep.
No pain he causes when he comes in sleep
Gently to steal our hearts from where we lie.

* i.e. to the preceding poem, 'Dante to Love's Faithful'

He stole your heart when she you worship was
Falling – he had perceived it – into death;
And fearing this, he gave it her to eat.

You saw him leave in sorrow then, because
Sweet sleep was on the point of ending with
The imperious advent of its opposite.

FROM THE GERMAN OF RAINER MARIA RILKE (1875–1926)

Archaic Torso of Apollo

Not to be known, the inconceivable
Head that the eyes ripened in. Yet the torso
Is like a branching gas-lamp, glowing still,
In which his gaze, no more than turned down low,

Burns on, gleams. Else it could not dazzle so,
The curved swell of the chest; nor could there be
In the slight twist of the loins a smile that goes
Toward the fulcrum that was potency.

Else the stone would appear disfigured, lopped,
Beneath the shoulders' lucid plunge and rush
And would not glisten like a wild beast's pelt;

And would not from its proper contours thus
Break like a star: for there is nowhere safe
From being seen here. You must change your life.

'Say, poet, what it is you do'

Say, poet, what it is you do. – *I praise.*
How can you look into the monster's gaze
And accept what has death in it? – *I praise.*
But poet, the anonymous, and those
With no name, how do you call on them? – *I praise.*
What right have you though, in each changed disguise,
In each new mask, to trust your truth? – *I praise.*
Both calm and violent things know you for theirs,
Both star and storm: how so? *Because I praise.*

*FROM THE PORTUGUESE OF FERNANDO PESSOA
(1888–1935)*

'I leave to the blind and deaf'

I leave to the blind and deaf
The soul with boundaries,
For I would feel all things
In all manner of ways.

I muse on earth and heaven
From heights of consciousness –
Innocent: for my eyes
Glimpse nothing I possess.

But I see, so intently –
Dispersed through what I see –
That in each thought I am,
At once, a different me.

And as those things are fragments
Of being in dispersion,
I split my soul up, each
Portion a different person.

And if I see my soul
With another view,
I ask, Is that a basis
For judgement that holds true?

Ah, just as for land and sea
And boundless sky. He errs
Who thinks himself his own.
Not mine, I am diverse.

Let me – if things are fragments
Of universal mind –
Be the pieces of myself,
Various, undefined.

If all I feel is other
And self apart from me,
How did the soul's end
Become identity?

Thus I conform to what
God's made from the first days;
God's way is different
And I am different ways.

Thus I ape God, who when
He made what is, withdrew
Infinity from it
And even oneness too.

'There was a rhythm in my sleep'

There was a rhythm in my sleep.
I have lost it – when I woke it went.
Why did I ever lead my life
Away from self-abandonment?

What was it, that which was not? I
Know that it lulled me sweetly then,
As though the very lulling sought
To make me who I am again.

Music there was which, when I woke
From dreaming it, broke off. The link,
Though, did not die: the theme goes on
In what impels me not to think.

from *The Keeper of Flocks*
by 'Alberto Caeiro'

IX

I am a keeper of flocks.
The flock is my thoughts
And my thoughts are all sensations.
I think with my eyes and with my ears
And with my hands and feet
And with my nose and mouth.

Thinking a flower is to see it and smell it
And eating a fruit is to taste its meaning.

That's why, on a hot day,
When I feel sad at so much delight,
And I stretch out on the grass
And close my warm eyes,
I feel my whole body stretched out in what's real,
I know the truth and I'm happy.

X

'Hey, keeper of flocks,
You, there at the roadside,
What does the wind tell you, passing by?'

'That it's the wind, and that it passes,
And that it's already passed before,
And that it'll pass again.
And what does it say to you?'

'A great deal more than that.
It speaks of so much more to me.
Of memories and desires
And of things that never were.'

'You've never heard the wind passing.
Wind is all that the wind speaks of.
What you heard it say was a lie,
And the lie is your own.'

'You who, believing in your Christs and Marys'
by 'Ricardo Reis'

You who, believing in your Christs and Marys,
Trouble the limpid waters of my spring,
      And do so but to tell me
      That other kinds of water

In better times bathe meadows somewhere else –
Why speak to me of other realms if these
      Meadows and streams delight me
      And are of here and now?

The gods gave this reality, and gave it
This outwardness to make it real indeed.
      What are my dreams, if not
      Handiwork of the gods?

Leave me Reality, that is of the moment –
Also my tranquil and immediate gods
　　　Who do not live in Vagueness
　　　But in fields, and in rivers.

Let life go by for me in pagan fashion
To the accompaniment of slender pipes
　　　Whereby the reedy banks
　　　Of streams acknowledge Pan.

Live in your dreams and leave to me the deathless
Altars whereon I make observances,
　　　Leave me the seen presence
　　　Of gods who are most near.

You who court vainly what excels this life,
Leave life to those with faith in something older
　　　Than Christ upon his cross
　　　And Mary weeping.

Comfort me, Ceres, lady of the fields,
Apollo, Venus, and archaic Uranus,
　　　And thunderbolts, compelling,
　　　Being from the hand of Jove.

FROM THE POLISH OF CZESŁAW MIŁOSZ (1911–2004)

From a Notebook: Bon on Lake Geneva

Copper beeches, glistening poplars
And pine-trees steep above the October fog.
In the valley the lake steams. On the other side,
On mountain ridges, snow already lies.
What remains of life? Only this light,
Peculiar to sunny weather in this season,

Which makes you blink. People say: This *is* –
And there is neither skill nor talent
Able to reach beyond whatever *is*,
And unnecessary memories lose their strength.

A smell of cider in barrels. The priest
Mixes lime with a spade outside the school.
By a path my son is running there. Boys carry
Sacks of chestnuts they have gathered from the slopes.
If I forget thee, O Jerusalem
(Saith the prophet), let my right hand wither.
An underground tremor shatters that which is:
Mountains crack, forests are rent asunder.
Touched by what was and by what will be,
What *is* crumbles into dust.
Violent, clean, the world is again in ferment,
And neither ambition nor memory will cease.

Autumn skies, who are the same in childhood,
The same in manhood and old age, I shall
Not look at you. And landscapes,
Who nourish the human heart with gentle warmth,
What poison is in you that lips are numb,
And arms folded across the chest, and eyes
Like a drowsy animal's. But whoever in what is
Finds peace, order and an eternal moment
Will vanish without trace. Do you agree then
To destroy what is and snatch the eternal moment
From flux – a gleam on the black river? I do.

Translated with George Gömöri

FROM THE BULGARIAN OF LYUBOMIR NIKOLOV (b. 1954)

A Wasp

I had only half-opened one of the window's wings
                                    Ovid, *Amores*

High over our bed, a wasp.

And this slim Egyptian queen
is dancing in the hot air,
spinning, vibrating in a sunbeam,
whizzing between the curtains, swooping,
circling the downy quince,
then rising again, buzzing, drifting on air,
and tracing yellow circles around the quince,
till all of a sudden the head thrusts deep
into the fruit's tunnel.

The whole body wants to squeeze into it…

Wants to get wings and sting and all
into the darkness.
To suck tart juice with the proboscis
and, sunk into the damp womb,
to dart in it like lightning,
to reach as far down as the oozy pip,
that we might hear it booming
like the Deluge with its awesome waves, and later
erupting from the darkness a limpid drop
will moisten the flattened down.

Translated with Viara Tcholakova

Hornets

From the hollowed heads of sunflowers
my father has made a bonfire in the garden.
And hornets, having smelt the sun,
come down upon him in their angry swarms.
He wants victory over them.
The fire keeps growing, licking the stars,
the monsters beat their wings of darkness
and the flames sting their bellies.
Some of them, almost burnt, must drag
their smoking, wingless bodies through the grass,
expiring on the damp covers
in damp sheets of dew.
Their wicked seed is wiped out almost.
My father gleefully rubs his hands
but from time to time a bee flits by
to be lost in the flames forever:
one small bee less to return to the hive…
Until morning, my father will toss in fever.
When the sun crawls up out of the earth –
the burning body of a bee.

Translated with Viara Tcholakova

Scaling Carp

Slowly the knife's grown over with blood and scales.
I grasp it tight, I flay
and try not to meet the eyes
of these mute creatures.
I flay just as I'd shave
pig's skin – against the bristle.
I take off the golden armour
to see their shining bodies underneath –
sleek, soft, naked.
On my shirt and my trousers, scales.

They fly about me like wet chaff,
coating my face and shoes.
And I remember an old ikon:
the dry gully, the two butterflies,
the dragon
pinned to the ground by St George's lance,
the small dog with the pink tongue
licking the dark clots.
Beside me, a bowl of flour –
I dredge the fish in it.
Through their white shirts
break blue ribs of blood.
It's noon.

And the oil's already boiling.

Translated with the poet

St George's Day

Blood glistens on the knife.
The lamb hangs flayed, its hide
an inch off. Over it,
cherry blossoms. Wasps.

Initiate so soon
into death's mystery.
Now from its severed head
an angel's eye regards us.

Translated with Viara Tcholakova

Hagia Sophia

Hagia Sophia – the Lord decreed that here
Emperors and peoples should stop short!
Your cupola, one eyewitness will swear,
Hangs by a flawless chain from heaven's vault.

A mark for times to come, Justinian
Took from Diana's shrine at Ephesus
A hundred and seven columns of green stone
For strange new gods, to which she acquiesced.

But what was in your builder's mind, when he,
Lavish in gift, lofty in thought and sense,
Disposed the apses and the exedrae
To east and west, aligned like compass points?

A radiant temple bathing in the world:
The light of forty windows shines supreme,
With four great archangels – finest of all –
On pendentives descending from the dome.

Of spheres and wisdom formed, it will out-gleam
Peoples and centuries, as it has of old,
And resonating sobs from seraphim
Cannot corrode that dark veneer of gold.

NOTES AND INDEX

NOTES

My poems are sometimes allusive and often include quotations and references. I have only included these in the notes which follow when it seemed to me that the reader's understanding would be otherwise restricted, or when I felt an acknowledgement was required. C.W.

p. 6 *The Invalid Storyteller.* An extract from a narrative sequence now discarded. It is spoken by a group of people who, as children, paid regular visits to an aged invalid, who told them tragic stories. At the end of the sequence the invalid dies.

p. 20 *In Malignant Times.* Inspired by some seventeenth-century epitaphs in the Priory Church of St Bartholomew-the-Great, Smithfield. One of them is for James Rivers, who died in 1641, the year before the outbreak of the Civil War:

> Within this hollow vault here rests the frame
> Of that high soul wch late inform'd the same
> Torn from the service of the state in's prime
> By a Disease malignant as the time
> Who's life and death designd no other end
> Than to serve God his Country & his friend
> Who when Ambytyon Tyrany & Pride
> Conquer'd the Age, Conquer'd Hymself & dyd

The German epigraph is from Martin Luther's hymn, 'A safe stronghold our Lord is still', a paraphrase of Psalm 46.

p. 22 *Sanctuary.* When the Huns and the Lombards invaded Northern Italy, the Veneti sought refuge on the islands of the lagoon. One of these islands, Torcello, was their commercial centre until it was superseded by the city of Venice. The islands were vulnerable to attack, both from the Lombards on the mainland and from Barbary pirates at sea. The poem is indebted to the 'Torcello' chapter of John Ruskin's *The Stones of Venice*.

p. 23 *The Disenchanted.* John Atkinson Grimshaw (1836–1893) was a painter of atmospheric urban scenes. *Liverpool Quay by Moonlight* is in Tate Britain, London.

p. 25 *Saxon Buckle.* The Anglo-Saxon hoard known as the Sutton Hoo treasure dates from the seventh century. Excavated in Suffolk in 1939, it is now in the British Museum, London. The belt buckle is in the form of an endless knot of gold interlace. The gold is further decorated with abstract bestial heads, carved and with niello inlay. Looked at overall, the buckle resembles the head of a horned animal, with its three rivets suggesting eyes and nose. The treasure was buried with an Anglian ruler, probably Rædwald, King of East Anglia.

p. 32 *On the Demolition of the 'Kite' District.* The Kite was a modest residential district of central Cambridge, which suffered for several years from planning blight. Much of it was finally demolished in the spring of 1980.

p. 41 *On the Devil's Dyke.* The dyke is a large earthwork, about 7½ miles in length, near the Cambridgeshire–Suffolk border. It is thought to have been built to defend the kingdom of East Anglia against incursions along the Icknield Way.

p. 47 *The Natural History of the Rook.* This poem includes quotations from Charles Waterton's *Essays on Natural History.* Waterton (1772–1865) turned his estate at Walton Hall, Yorkshire, into what can now be regarded as the world's first wildlife sanctuary.

p. 49 *Home.* A fairly free translation from the Italian poet and novelist, Cesare Pavese (1908–50).

p. 50 *Homecoming.* This sequence pursues a theme through three German-language poets of the twentieth century: the German Georg Heym (1887–1912), the Austrian Georg Trakl (1887–1914) and the Romanian Paul Celan (1920–70). The translations are not faithful.

p. 51 *For the Fly-Leaf of a King James Bible.* The epigraph is quoted from Friedrich Hölderlin's 'Brot und Wein' [Bread and Wine]. Reflecting on the absence of the gods from the modern world, Hölderlin asks: 'What use are poets in a needy time?'

p. 52 *Antiphonal Sonnets.* John Taverner (c.1495–1545) was a composer of polyphonic church music. After his conversion to Protestantism, he seems to have renounced musical activity and was employed by Thomas Cromwell in the spoliation of the monasteries. The first of these sonnets refers to his motet *Dum transisset sabbatum,* a setting of Mark 16.1–2. The second alludes to a letter from Taverner to Cromwell: 'according to your Lordship's commandment the Rood was burned the seventh day'.

p. 54 *To Nicholas Hawksmoor.* All the buildings named in the poem were designed or include work by the architect Nicholas Hawksmoor

(1661–1736). All Souls is the Oxford College, but Christ Church is the parish church of Spitalfields in the East End of London.

p. 58 *The Peaceable Kingdom.* In the Golden Age, wrote Fulke Greville, 'The laws were inward that did rule the heart' (*Caelica* XLIV).

p. 61 *Prayer for my Children.* This is loosely based on the sixth-century Evening Hymn 'Te lucis ante terminum', part of which is quoted in Canto VIII of Dante's *Purgatorio.*

pp. 67 *Invocation.* The Venerable Bede, in his *Ecclesiastical History of the English People,* tells the story of the poet Caedmon, who was a herdsman and lay brother at the Abbey of Whitby in the seventh century. According to Bede, Caedmon would slip out of hall after dinner to avoid being called upon to sing to the harp at table. One night when he was sleeping with the cattle, an angel appeared to him in a dream and told him to sing of how God made the world. This is the origin, Bede tells us, of the nine-line poem known as Caedmon's Hymn, the earliest poem by a known author in any dialect of English.

p. 68 *Three Brueghel Paintings.* In the Kunsthistorisches Museum, Vienna.

p. 70 *The San Damiano Crucifix.* In St Bonaventura's *Life of St Francis* we learn how the Saint embarked on his ministry. As he knelt in prayer in the ruined church of San Damiano, he heard a voice from the painted crucifix over the altar. 'Francis,' it said, 'go and repair my house, which, as you can see, is falling into utter ruin.' Soon afterwards St Francis began the task of rebuilding what Bonaventura calls 'the material church'.

p. 74 *The Infinite Variety.* The Moghul Emperor Shah Jahan (1592–1666) was a patron of miniature painting.

p. 81 *Post-war Childhoods.* Simone Weil (1909–1943) was a French mystic, philosopher and social activist. Working in England for the French Resistance, she was diagnosed with tuberculosis. She died after refusing special treatment and restricting her diet to what she believed available to people in occupied France. *La Pesanteur et la grâce* is a posthumous collection of her austerely beautiful aphorisms.

'Fireweed' is a popular name for rosebay willowherb, which grows freely on land affected by fires.

p. 89 *Work.* A tribute to two great thinkers about art and literature, who both wrote about stone carving: Donald Davie, to whom it is dedicated, and John Ruskin. The carving described in part 2 is to be found in the Chapter House of Southwell Minster, Nottinghamshire. The carvings of leaves in that room represent the highest achievement of English Gothic sculpture in the thirteenth century. Davie's poem 'To a Brother in the Mystery' was inspired by them.

p. 91 *The Law of the House.* Canto XLV from *The Cantos of Ezra Pound* begins with the lines 'With Usura / Hath no man a house of good stone'.

p. 93 *At the Grave of William Morris.* Morris's grave was designed by his friend, the architect Philip Webb, in imitation of an Icelandic tomb. It is shaped like a gabled roof. Morris, incidentally, was an atheist.

p. 94 *Fonte Branda in Siena.* The large rectangular basin of this fountain is sheltered by a Gothic roof, which keeps the water cool. In *Inferno* XXX, Dante meets Adamo da Brescia, an unrepentant forger of false coin. He is one of a series of damned souls who are guilty of what Ezra Pound calls 'economic crime' – of crime, that is, against the common weal. Adamo is suffering from eternal thirst, but asserts that, if he could see his enemies similarly punished, he would forgo the sight of Fonte Branda. The passage is alluded to in the closing paragraph of Ruskin's last book, his autobiography *Praeterita*, concluded in 1889. Despite the fact that it was composed in the lucid intervals between mental breakdowns, *Praeterita* is mostly serene in tone.

p. 108 *In the Greenwood.* In August 1987, a 27-year-old gun-collector named Michael Ryan shot a young woman dead in Savernake Forest. There was no obvious motive. That same day he killed fifteen other people, including his mother, in the nearby town of Hungerford. He ended by committing suicide.

pp. 113–15 *Caedmon of Whitby.* This was written for musical setting. The text is based on the translation of Bede's *Ecclesiastical History* by Thomas Stapleton (1565). See note for 'Invocation' above, p. 289.

p. 121 *Lindisfarne Sacked.* The Northumbrian abbey of Lindisfarne on Holy Island was sacked by Viking raiders in 793. The magnificent Lindisfarne Gospels, made in the abbey in the previous century, were spirited away to the mainland and so preserved. Other manuscripts of the same school must have perished in the flames.

p. 126 *Kaspar Hauser.* In 1828, a youth of about sixteen was found wandering in the streets of Nuremberg. Unable to speak, he bore a note which said: 'I want to be a horseman like my father.' When the local pastor taught him a little language, it emerged that he had been kept in a dark room – possibly a stable – for as long as he could remember and had never encountered human society before. In 1833 he died a violent death; it is assumed that he was murdered, though he may have committed suicide.

p. 133 *Letter to J.A. Cuddon*. J.A. Cuddon (1928–96), known to his friends as Charles, was a writer, traveller and schoolmaster. His publications include five novels, two dictionaries and two travel books: *The Owl's Watchsong: A Study of Istanbul* (1957) and *The Companion Guide to Jugoslavia* (1968). Passionately interested in the theatre, he directed a production of Harold Pinter's *The Dumb Waiter* at Emanuel School, Wandsworth, in 1962. His schoolboy actors were the dramatist Steve Gooch and myself.

p. 144 *The Heron*. This is loosely based on a poem by the Spanish poet Juan del Encina (1468–1529/30).

pp. 145–6 *Vacations* and *To Pyrrha*. Both these poems are based on poems by Horace (*Odes* 1.9 and 1.5). 'Vacations' is too free to be called a translation.

p. 153 *Fernando Pessoa's Lisbon*. See the note on Pessoa below, p. 296.

p. 155 *A Baroque Concerto*. Edgar Bowers (1924–2000) was, for me, one of the great poets of modern times. My sonnet refers to two groups of poems by him: the poems in his first book *The Form of Loss* (1956), which draw on his experiences as an American soldier in Germany at the end of the Second World War, and 'Thirteen Views of Santa Barbara', a sequence of poems he wrote in the 1980s about civic order and the natural environment in Southern California, the region where he spent most of his professional life. His *Collected Poems* was published by Knopf in 1997.

p. 156 *Casa Natal de Borges*. Written after visiting the birthplace of Jorge Luis Borges in Buenos Aires.

p. 157 *The Translator's Apology*. The first line of this poem is based on a line of Ezra Pound's, which itself parodies the refrain of a poem by Ernest Dowson. My poem was sparked off when the poet Patrick McGuinness jokingly quoted Pound's line at a conference on translation

p. 166 *The Ruin*. Andrei Rublyov (or Rublev) (c.1360–1427/30) was the greatest of all Russian ikon painters. His ikon of Christ, *The Saviour*, is the only surviving panel of a lost ikonostasis and now hangs in the Tretyakov Gallery in Moscow. For Miklós Radnóti, see below, p. 293.

p. 167 *Much Ado about Nothing*. John Kerrigan, in his edition of Shakespeare's sonnets, calls 'nothing' a 'very Shakespearean quantity'. This poem consists almost entirely of quotations, most of them instances of that Shakespearean obsession. The two Middle English quotations are from the fourteenth-century treatise on contemplation, *The Cloud of Unknowing*, the second of them interwoven with a line from 'The Snow Man' by Wallace Stevens.

p. 168 *The Holy of Holies*. The Temple in Jerusalem was destroyed by the Romans under Titus in AD 70. This poem borrows from the account of that disaster by the Romano-Jewish historian Josephus, who witnessed it himself.

pp. 171–2 *The Ladder*. Lines 12-15 borrow from a passage in Dante's *Vita Nuova*, as translated by Dante Gabriel Rossetti: 'I have spoken of Love as though it were a thing outward and visible: not only [as] a spiritual essence, but as a bodily substance also. The which thing, in absolute truth, is a fallacy…'

pp. 175–6 *Chutney* and *The Apple Trees*. For Lyubomir Nikolov, see below, p. 296.

p. 182 *W.S. Graham Reading*. This recalls Graham's reading at the Cambridge Poetry Festival in 1981.

p. 183 *The Falls*. Written after a visit to the Finger Lakes and Niagara Falls in upstate New York. I had recently visited the Museum of Modern Art in New York City, where I saw Jackson Pollock's *One*, perhaps the greatest of his 'drip paintings'. This poem makes extensive use of quotation and allusion. It borrows notably from Gerard Manley Hopkins, Ruskin, Dante, Henry Vaughan and St Paul.

p. 190 *Stigmata*. The Stigmata are the five wounds of Christ. This sequence also refers to two saints who are said to have received the Stigmata in their own bodies: St Francis of Assisi and, in the twentieth century, the Capuchin friar Padre Pio.

p. 190 *The Visit to La Verna*. The Franciscan monastery on Mount La Verna in Tuscany includes the place where, according to tradition, St Francis received the Stigmata. A year later the Saint died. Various relics associated with him can be seen in the monastery; these include his sackcloth habit. In a cave under the monastery there is an oblong grid, where the saint is thought to have slept.

p. 191 *A Quotation*. The italicised line is quoted from my poem 'Two Journals', p. 102.

pp. 196–8 *Piero's 'Resurrection'*. The fresco of the Resurrection by Piero della Francesca (c.1419/21–1492) was painted in the Palazzo Comunale of the artist's home town, Sansepolcro in Tuscany. Kenneth Clark found the painting to be more pagan than Christian.

p. 200 *The Need for Angels*. The story of Dante drawing an angel is from the *Vita Nuova*. 'Teresa' is both St Teresa of Ávila (1515–82), who had a vision of an angel plunging a spear into her heart, and Thérèse Neumann (1898–1962), another modern stigmatic. The cinema referred to is purely circumstantial.

p. 217 *Shakespeare*. This poem is in memory of the schoolteacher who, when I was eight, encouraged me to read Shakespeare. Her name, Eleanor E. Inkpen, provoked some hilarity, but there have been few people in my life to whom I owe more.

p. 217 *Brook's 'Lear'*. Peter Brook's production of *King Lear*, with Paul Scofield in the title role, was first performed at Stratford in 1962. It transferred to London for the winter season, and I saw it there as a sixth-former. Brook cut two or three small but significant details from the play. One was the removal of Edmund after his death, which meant that the body stayed on stage till the end of the play.

p. 220 *Civitas*. The title is Latin for 'civilisation'. 'Martlet': either a house martin or, in heraldry, a small songbird. ALF: Animal Liberation Front.

p. 225 *A Valedictory Ode*. During the Middle Ages and the Renaissance, a period when women were denied formal education, six Cambridge colleges were founded by women.
   Line 13: 'whose connections'. Sidney Sussex College, Cambridge, was founded in 1596 by Frances, Countess of Sussex. The Countess was aunt to Sir Philip Sidney and his sister, Mary, Countess of Pembroke, joint authors of *The Sidney Psalter*. Mary's sons, William and Philip, were patrons of Shakespeare and his company, and the family was distantly related to that of George Herbert, whose mother Lady Magdalen Herbert was a friend and patron of John Donne's.

p. 231 *Jenő Dsida* (1907–38) was the outstanding Hungarian poet from Transylvania during the interwar period. He lived most of his life in Kolozsvár, where he worked as a journalist. His best poetry shows the influence of Expressionism. There are four of his poems in the anthology *The Colonnade of Teeth*, eds. George Gömöri and George Szirtes (Bloodaxe, 1996).

pp. 231–45 *Miklós Radnóti* (1910–44) is one of Hungary's outstanding poets. Of Jewish origin, he became an ethical Socialist and a Roman Catholic. Though influenced by Romantic and Modernist writing, he shows in his mature poetry a dedication to European classicism. For most of the Second World War he was interned in labour camps in Serbia. In 1944 he and his fellow internees were force-marched back into Hungary, where most of them were shot by firing-squad and buried in a mass grave. Radnóti's body was subsequently identified by a notebook of poems in his greatcoat pocket. See *Forced March: Selected Poems*, translated by Clive Wilmer and George Gömöri (Enitharmon Press, 2003).

p. 231 *Garden on Istenhegy*. Istenhegy is a hill on the steep Buda side of Budapest.

p. 233 *First Eclogue*. The first of a cycle of eight Eclogues composed between 1938 and 1944. The epigraph is from the *Georgics* of Virgil: 'For right and wrong are inverted here: there are so many wars that overrun the world, so many shapes of wickedness.'

The poem refers to the final stage of the Spanish Civil War, when the Republican forces were driven north into the Pyrenees. 'Federico' is the great Spanish poet Federico García Lorca, who was shot by Nationalists in 1936. Radnóti identified with Lorca and anticipated a similar fate for himself.

'[O]ur beloved Attila' is Attila József, the modern Hungarian poet most admired by Radnóti. ('Attila' is stressed on the first syllable.) A persistent critic of 'the present state' – i.e. the right-wing regime of Admiral Horthy – József committed suicide in 1937.

p. 235 *Written in a Copy of 'Steep Path'*. A collection of Radnóti's poems, published in 1938. The execution of Lorca stands behind this poem too.

p. 241 *Eighth Eclogue*. Written in 1944, shortly before German troops evacuated the Serbian camps where Radnóti was interned. Some of the Prophet's lines are taken more or less verbatim from prophetic books in the Bible: see in particular Nahum 1 and 3, Habbakkuk 2 and Isaiah 6. I have used the King James Bible where Radnóti used that of Gáspár Károli (1590).

p. 243 *Forced March*. Written on the march which the poem seeks to evoke. 'Fanni' was Radnóti's wife.

p. 244 *Postcards*. Also written on the forced march. The poems follow the route of the marchers from Serbia through Hungary and towards the German border. The last of them was written nine days before Radnóti was shot by firing squad.

'*Der springt noch auf*': 'That one can still get up' – presumably the words of a German guard. In the event, the poet was executed by Hungarians.

p. 245 *István Vas* (1910–91) was a friend of Radnóti's. His work, very much associated with urbanity and the city of Budapest, is strongly affected by the identification of many metropolitan Hungarians with Western European culture, in particular that of France and Britain. As a celebrated translator of Shakespeare, Keats and T.S. Eliot, Vas was very much of the Anglophile tendency. See *Through the Smoke: Selected Poems*, ed. Miklós Vajda (Corvina, 1989).

Romanus Sum – 'I am a Roman'. The Roman chronicler Livy tells many legends of the heroic early days of Republican Rome. One of these concerns a young Roman known to history as Mucius Scaevola. When the Etruscan king Lars Porsenna gave orders for Mucius to be burnt alive, Mucius thrust his own hand into the flames, giving no sign of pain. Impressed by the young man's courage, Porsenna freed him. Vas uses the story as a parable of Hungarian politics in the post-war period.

pp. 246–50 *János Pilinszky* (1921–81) served with the Hungarian army in World War II. His second book, *Harmadnapon* (On the Third Day, 1959), established him as a courageous witness to the horrors of mid-twentieth-century Europe. It also registered the presence of an austerely economical poet with the outlook of a Christian Existentialist. See *Selected Poems*, translated by Ted Hughes and János Csokits (Carcanet, 1976), and a pamphlet, *Passio: Thirteen Poems*, translated by Clive Wilmer and George Gömöri (Worple, 2011).

pp. 250–52 *György (George) Gömöri* was born in Budapest in 1934, and is passionately attached to his native city. In 1956, however, he was obliged to flee to Britain because of his active role in the failed Hungarian uprising of that year. For many years he taught Polish and Hungarian literature at Cambridge, retiring in 2001. He has been a key figure in the translation and dissemination of Hungarian poetry in English since the late 1960s. See *Polishing October: Selected Poems*, translated by Clive Wilmer and George Gömöri (Shoestring Press, 2008).

pp. 252–3 *Domokos Szilágyi* (1938–76) was a Hungarian poet from Transylvania who lived both in Bucharest and in Kolozsvár. His work combines the traditions of Hungarian poetry with the formal innovations of the *avant-garde*. There are three of his poems in the anthology *The Colonnade of Teeth*, eds. George Gömöri and George Szirtes (Bloodaxe, 1996).

Ivan Meštrović (1883–1962) was a Croatian sculptor of mainly religious subjects.

pp. 254–61 *György Petri* (1943–2000) is the most striking poet of the post-Modernist era in Hungary. A person of anarchistic temperament, he was the fiercest of the literary dissidents who attacked the Communist regime in its last phase – the era of liberal 'goulash' Communism. Contemporary European literature has few satirists to equal him for the savagery of his criticism and the resourcefulness of his imagination. See *Eternal Monday: Selected Poems*, translated by Clive Wilmer and George Gömöri (Bloodaxe, 1999).

p. 257 *To Imre Nagy*. Nagy was Prime Minister of Hungary from October to November 1956. His was the reformist government that briefly attempted to resist Soviet power in Hungary. The poem alludes to the evening before the Soviet invasion when Nagy, on the point of taking office, sought unsuccessfully to calm his supporters in the street outside Parliament. In 1958 he was tried *in camera* and hanged in a prison yard on the outskirts of Budapest.

p. 258 *Daydreams. Sors bona nihil aliud*: a Latin motto well-known in Hungary. It means roughly: 'Good fortune is all you need'.

p. 259 *A Recognition*. Written on the fall of Communism in 1989.

pp. 261–5 *Anna T. Szabó* (born 1972) is a Hungarian poet and translator of Transylvanian origin. She has published five books of poetry and several books of translations, including my own *Végtelen változatok* [The Infinite Variety] (Szeged, 2002), translated with George Gömöri. She writes with acute sensitivity about the joys and sorrows of a woman's life. English translations of her poems are included in the anthology *New Order*, ed. George Szirtes (Arc Publishers, 2009).

pp. 274–8 *Fernando Pessoa* (1888–1935) was a Portuguese writer of verse and prose – one of the greatest European poets of the twentieth century. Pessoa's theme is identity, its fissiparousness and the various modes of escape from it. This is reflected in his adoption of different personalities, such that the authorship of his poetry is divided between 'Fernando Pessoa' and three heteronyms – Alberto Caeiro, Ricardo Reis and Álvaro de Campos. Caeiro and Reis, unlike 'Pessoa', are both neo-pagans, though they have little else in common. Caeiro is an uneducated peasant, Reis a sophisticated doctor with classical tastes.

pp. 280–83 *Lyubomir Nikolov* (born 1954) is a Bulgarian poet who now lives in the United States. His poetry, which has an almost oriental compactness, springs from an intense attachment to the landscapes and customs of his homeland and the remains that have been found there. It conveys an acute sense of transience at the same time as a feeling for the past's enduring presence in daily life. See *Pagan*, translated by Roland Flint and Viara Tcholakova (Carnegie Mellon, 1992) and *Unreal Estate*, translated by Miroslav Nikolov (Carnegie Mellon, 2009).

p. 283 *Hagia Sophia*. The great fourth-century basilica in Constantinople. The name means 'Holy Wisdom' and is pronounced 'Aya Sofía'. For Diana and her temple, see the story of St Paul at Ephesus in Acts 19.

INDEX OF TITLES AND FIRST LINES

(Titles are printed in italics, first lines in roman.)